Samuel Rutherford has deservedly attra[...]
Lex Rex was controversial enough in its [...]
the order of the civil authority and is see[...]
political theories. The 350th anniversar[...]
reminded many of the leadership of Ruth[...] presbyterian
polity. But Rutherford is a complex figure. The erotic imagery of his *Letters*
of pastoral counsel contrasts sharply with the scholastic style of *Lex Rex*.
He described himself as a man of extremes. Kingsley Rendell's study
provides the welcome service of putting this important and interesting figure
in the context of his times and of the church controversies in which he was
involved.

William S. Barker
Westminster Theological Seminary
Philadelphia, Pennsylvania

This is a very timely book, for if ever the Church was in need of another
Rutherford, or at least of being reminded of what he stood for, then the time
is certainly now. How many today would be willing to preach if they were
aware, as Rutherford was, of the price they would pay for such Christ-centred
preaching as he was 'guilty' of? Rendell is right when he admits that
Rutherford will remain something of an enigma, but what he does achieve
well is to bring to life the many facets that make up this remarkable divine:
Pastor, Prisoner, Reformer, Apologist, and Protester. The book is
interestingly written and well researched, but more than merely imparting
information about one of the real jewels of the Scottish Church, the reader
is challenged by the life and devotion and self-denial that were characteristic
of Samuel Rutherford. Such challenges will always transcend denominational
barriers.

Dr Michael McMullen
Midwestern Baptist Seminary
Kansas City, Missouri

Readers who know little of the course of the life of Samuel Rutherford in its
tangled and political context will find a reliable guide in Kingsley Rendell.
This is no uncritical hagiography of a writer whose complexity he himself
recognized – 'made up of extremes', as he described himself. Those who
have never encountered this relentless controversialist and this master-
wordsmith in sensual biblical imagery – both in one person – should start
here.

David Wright
Department of Ecclesiastical History
University of Edinburgh

Dr Kingsley Rendell was trained as a teacher at St. Luke's College, Exeter, in Religious Education. He obtained a distinction in the Archbishop's Examination in Divinity. From college he went directly into the Royal Navy being commissioned as an Observer in the Fleet Air Arm. On demobilisation in 1946, he read History at Glasgow University, graduating with honours in 1950 and studied for the Baptist ministry at the Baptist Theological College of Scotland. He served as minister in Cathcart (Glasgow), Sherborne, Montacute and New Whittington Baptist churches. From 1964 until 1976 Dr Rendell was Head of Department of Religious Studies at Totley College of Education, Sheffield and on retirement was invited to become minister of Maybole Baptist Church, a post he held until 1986, thereafter being made Minister Emeritus. Sadly, Dr Rendell died before this book was published. He leaves behind his wife Margaret, son Charles, daughter-in-law Joy and grandchildren Ailsa and Alexander.

SAMUEL RUTHERFORD

A NEW BIOGRAPHY OF
THE MAN & HIS MINISTRY

————— BY —————

KINGSLEY G· RENDELL

CHRISTIAN FOCUS

Christian Focus Publications
publishes books for all ages

Our mission statement –

STAYING FAITHFUL
In dependence upon God we seek to help make His infallible word, the Bible, relevant. Our aim is to ensure that the Lord Jesus Christ is presented as the only hope to obtain forgiveness of sin, live a useful life and look forward to heaven with Him.

REACHING OUT
Christ's last command requires us to reach out to our world with His gospel. We seek to help fulfill that by publishing books that point people towards Jesus and help them develop a Christ-like maturity. We aim to equip all levels of readers for life, work, ministry and mission.

Books in our adult range are published in three imprints.

Christian Focus contains popular works including biographies, commentaries, basic doctrine, and Christian living. Our children's books are also published in this imprint.

Mentor focuses on books written at a level suitable for Bible College and seminary students, pastors, and other serious readers. The imprint includes commentaries, doctrinal studies, examination of current issues, and church history.

Christian Heritage contains classic writings from the past.

© Christian Focus Publications 2003

ISBN 1 85792 262 X

Published in 2003 by
Christian Focus Publications, Geanies House, Fearn,
Ross-shire, IV20 1TW, Scotland

www.christianfocus.com

Cover design by Alister MacInnes

Printed and bound by
Mackays of Chatham

Contents

EDITOR'S NOTE

In the providence of God Kingsley Rendell did not live to see his biographical study of Samuel Rutherford through to publication. My task as editor has been to add a number of footnotes which provide fuller explanations of various matters, such as names and events, which may not be as familiar to readers as the author expected. At a few points the text has been corrected but otherwise the book is as Kingsley Rendell wrote it. This is Kingsley Rendell's book, not mine. May it serve to make a faithful minister of Jesus Christ better known to a new generation of readers and challenge them to follow the God of Samuel Rutherford with the zeal which he manifested.

David McKay
Reformed Theological College, Belfast

CHRONOLOGY OF RUTHERFORD'S LIFE

1600   Probable year of Rutherford's birth.

1617   Enters the University of Edinburgh.

1621   Receives the degree of Master of Arts.

1623   Appointed Regent of Humanity in the university.

1626   Rutherford is removed from his post on the ground of fornication with Euphan Hamilton, whom he subsequently marries.

1627   After studying theology, Rutherford becomes minister in Anwoth in Galloway.

1630   Rutherford's wife Euphan dies.

1636   Publishes *Exercitationes Apologeticae pro Divina Gratia*. On this account he is summoned in July to appear before the High Commission in Edinburgh, where he is forbidden to exercise his ministry and exiled to Aberdeen.

1637   On 23 July the first use of "Laud's Liturgy" sparks a riot in St. Giles' Cathedral, Edinburgh.

1638   *February*: Returns to Anwoth. On 23 February the National Covenant is signed in Greyfriars Churchyard in Edinburgh. *November*: Serves as a commissioner at the General Assembly in Glasgow.

1639   Appointed Professor of Divinity at the University of St. Andrews.

1640   Marries Jean McMath.

1642   Publishes *A Peaceable and Temperate Plea for Paul's Presbyterie in Scotland* .

1643   Appointed one of the Commissioners of the Church of Scotland to the Westminster Assembly as a consequence of the Solemn League and Covenant concluded in September.

1644   Publishes *Lex Rex* and *The Due Right of Presbyteries*.

1645   Publishes *The Trial and Triumph of Faith*.

1646   Publishes *The Divine Right of Church Government*.

1647   Publishes *Christ Dying and Drawing Sinners to Himself*. In
        November, returns to Scotland from the Westminster Assembly
        and becomes Principal of St. Mary's College, St. Andrews. Sides
        with the opponents of the Engagement.

1648   Publishes *A Survey of the Spiritual Antichrist*. On 17 August the
        Engagers are defeated by Cromwell at Preston.

1649   30 January: Charles I executed.
        Publishes *A Free Disputation against Pretended Liberty of
        Conscience*.

1650   On 3 September the Scots are defeated by Cromwell at Dunbar.

1651   1 January: Charles II crowned King at Scone by the Scots.
        Rutherford appointed Rector of the University of St. Andrews.
        Publishes *Disputatio Scholastica de Divina Providentia*. At the
        General Assembly in June, sides with the Protesters against the
        Resolutioners. On 3 September the Scots are defeated by Cromwell
        at Worcester. Charles flees to Europe.

1653   20 July: rival Resolutioner and Protester Assemblies in Edinburgh
        are dissolved by Cromwell's troops.

1655   Publishes *The Covenant of Life Opened*.

1658   Publishes *A Survey of the Survey of that Summe of Church Discipline*.

1659   Publishes *Influences of the Life of Grace*.

1660   *May*: Restoration of Charles II.
        October: copies of *Lex Rex* are publicly burned and Rutherford is
        stripped of all the posts he holds, including his pastoral charge. He
        is called to appear before the Committee of Estates to answer a charge
        of treason.

1661   29 March: dies and is buried at St. Andrews.

1664   Publication of *Joshua Redivivus*, the first collection of Rutherford's
        letters.

1668   Publication in Utrecht of *Examen Arminianismi*.

CHAPTER 1

STUDENT AND PROFESSOR

Although the lifespan of Samuel Rutherford does not fall strictly into the Covenanting period of Scottish history, the name of Rutherford will always be associated with the Covenant. Fame, perhaps, has not written it as indelibly upon the page of Scottish church history as those of Cameron, Cargill and Renwick, Covenanters of the succeeding generation, but Rutherford is none the less worthy of special study. His life and ministry provide an indispensable link between Andrew Melville and the Covenanters. It bridges the gap between the late sixteenth and mid-seventeenth centuries. There would have been no Covenanting torch to bear, if Rutherford and his associates had not kindled it in their day. Robert Gilmour aptly described him as 'a link in the evangelical succession of Christendom'.[1]

In the wake of the Reformation

Rutherford was born into the mêlée of the Scottish Reformation. It is understandable to think of the Reformation as centring in the ecclesiastical crisis of 1560. The dramatic events of that year, John Knox's sermon in St. John's Perth, the riot that ensued, and the subsequent rising of those who styled themselves 'the Faithful Congregation of Jesus Christ in Scotland', resulted in a sudden severance with Rome. The break with Rome, which was not so unexpected as is often imagined, was largely a negative act, which demanded positive measures if the schism was to be maintained, and a national reformed church established. The Church of Scotland, as we know it today, was not the brain child of Knox, but the result of growth from 1560 to 1689. As Professor Burleigh observed, 'What shape the Reformed Church of Scotland was to take was left an open question over which there was to be a long and bitter struggle. Not until 1689 can it be said to have been finally settled.'[2] In the words of T. C. Smout, 'It emerged as the

9

classic Presbyterian church of the eighteenth and nineteenth
centuries, with its elders, deacons, ministers and kirk session,
Presbyterian synods, and General Assembly.'[3]

During the first decade of the reformed faith in Scotland the
pressing problem was the spiritual care of the Scottish people.
Joseph Robertson's contention that the church was largely made
up of 'rich livings with the care of thousands of souls, held by
boys, by infants even, by men deformed in body, imbecile in mind,
hardened in ignorance, old in wickedness and sin'[4] may have been
something of an exaggeration, but it contains a sad truth. Knox,
who is generally recognised as a Father of the Scottish
Reformation, was not primarily concerned with theories of church
government, but with the parochial consideration of establishing
the reformed faith, and pastoring the flock of God in Scotland.
His concern was apostolic success rather than apostolic succession.
Unlike many who succeeded him, Knox followed Calvin, having
no objection to some form of Episcopacy. Professor G.D.
Henderson pointed out: 'the question of Presbyterian government
was not one that interested the reformers. No constitutional
document of the Reformation is concerned about it;'[5] while Smout
has observed that 'nothing in the polity of the Church can be
described as Presbyterian'.[6] Knox did not deny that national and
ecumenical organisation has its uses, but he insisted that the *esse*
of the church was to be found in the local congregation, where
there is true preaching of the Word of God, right administration
of the sacraments of Christ Jesus – and ecclesiastical discipline
uprightly ministered as God's Word prescribes.[7]

The Scottish Reformers were careful to distinguish between
Prelacy and Episcopacy.* In 1560 there was not so much reason
to resist Episcopacy as there was a century later. It was the
patronage of James VI and Charles I that made it so odious. Its
imposition by the Stuarts, largely for their own convenience, made
it unacceptable to the Scots. James Moffatt was of the opinion
that 'it might have proved stable. What upset it was the absolutism

*'Episcopacy' is government by church officers called 'bishops'. Different
systems accord varying powers to these bishops. 'Prelacy' is the state-
supported episcopal system characteristic of the Church of England.

of James and his son.'[8] When we remember that Knox was one of the six presbyters who, in the Confession of Faith of 1560, allowed for the appointment of superintendents, which to his opponents were bishops in all but name, there is justification in Donaldson's description of the early reformed church in Scotland as 'Independency with a dash of Episcopacy'.[9] Ross, in his *History of Congregational Independency in Scotland*, maintained that initially in the Scots Confession and the First Book of Discipline 1561, (both of which were largely drawn up by Knox), the ecclesiastical order was guided by 'the principles for which Independents have all along contended',[10] the polity of the reformation churches in Scotland being distinctly Independent and Congregational.[11]

Episcopacy can be detected too. After the Presbyterian system had been established, bishops, abbots and priors, many of whom were Protestants and laymen, were to be found throughout the country. In the assembly which met on December 25th, 1567, Knox himself was appointed to join the Superintendent of Lothian in his visitation from Stirling to Berwick, and thereafter to visit Kyle, Carrick and Cunningham.[12] In 1578 it was agreed by the civil and ecclesiastical authorities that the names and titles of archbishops and bishops should continue for those who now acted as superintendents, subject to the Kirk and General Assembly.

To this Knox raised no objections. What did raise his ire was the flow of church revenue into the hands of laymen, with consequent patronage, which was to vex the Church of Scotland for almost four centuries. Knox longed to see ecclesiastical revenues used to provide an adequate ministry, an efficient educational system, and relief of the poor. Out of the total revenue available, ultimately only one ninth went to the support of the national church, while clergy of the old regime were given two thirds of their revenue. Temporal lands of religious houses, by devious means, came into the possession of the nobles. Many reverted to the crown and were later lavished upon commendators or lay occupants of benefices (the 'Lords of Erection' as they were called), or on royal favourites. Many, however, were irretrievably lost as long leases and feus [a perpetual lease at a fixed rent], while some were appropriated by force. Dr. Malcolm Taylor, almost a century ago, rightly remarked that, 'far reaching as were the changes which the Reformation introduced, the practical organisation and beliefs which had been inherited from the past were recast in accordance with the ideas and altered conditions of the times, rather than exchanged for entirely new principles and methods'.[13]

Patently some clarification of ecclesiastical government and relation between church and state was necessary. The Regent Morton favoured a similar settlement to that which existed in England, the church being controlled by the supreme power of the Crown. He strongly supported Episcopacy, but was prepared to subject bishops to the will of the General Assembly. The Assembly of 1572 meeting at Leith drew up a Concordat – largely the work of Morton – which decreed that archbishoprics and bishoprics would be left as they were until the monarch attained his majority. Chapters should not be abolished, but their members be replaced by senior ministers as death depleted their numbers. Bishops were to be consecrated to vacant sees, and be required to take an oath of allegiance to the king. They were to be more than superintendents, but subject to the General Assembly; a conservative compromise with the ancient order. Morton had cause to be pleased, and followed up his success at Leith by securing the election of Douglas to the archbishopric of St. Andrews.

Knox was not opposed to some form of Episcopacy; indeed, he advised the filling of vacant bishoprics according to the agreement reached at Leith. But he had misgivings about Morton's policy, voicing them in his usual thunderous tones on the occasion of Douglas' institution to the see of St. Andrews. The aged Knox did not foresee that within a few years Morton would have filled all the vacancies with his own nominees, the 'Tulchan Bishops' as they were called. Nor did the reformer foresee that Morton would come to a profitable financial arrangement with the nearly senile Archbishop of St. Andrews. After the Leith Assembly, the way seemed open for the imposition of royal authority over the Church, and possibly its secularisation; but Morton had moved too far and too fast. The fear of 'popery' was aroused and no amount of explanation could remove it, even though Morton assumed the role of Court opponent and champion of the reformed faith.

The Contribution of Andrew Melville to the Reformation

In the spring of 1574, after an appeal from his nephew to raise the standard of education in Scotland, the Scottish exile Andrew Melville left Geneva for his native soil. He was destined not to make any significant contribution to Scottish education, but to play an important part in the drama of ecclesiastical politics. On arrival in Scotland he was offered a post in the household of Morton, but declined. After residing for three months with his brother, in November of that year he settled in Glasgow.

Melville's arrival in Scotland was most opportune for those who feared a Romeward drift. During his six years in Geneva, he had been greatly influenced by the thorough-going Presbyterianism of Beza. Melville was not the man to view the ecclesiastical situation of 1574 with indifference. He was strongly opposed to Episcopacy. He made his presence felt at the March General Assembly of the Kirk. John Durie, an Edinburgh minister, voicing the sentiments of Melville, asked 'if the bischopes, as they are now in Scotland, hes their functions of the Word of God or not, or if the Chapters appointit for creating of them, aucht to be tollerated in this reformed Kirk?'[14] Along with John Craige, James Lawsone, George Hay, John Row and David Lindsay, Melville was appointed to a Commission whose brief was to discuss the matters and report back to the Assembly. They thought it not expedient to answer to the question of bishops, only to decree that 'if any bischopes heis chosen who has fit qualities as the Word of God requires, let him be tried by the Generall Assembly *de novo*, and so deposit'.[15]

The General Assembly under the influence of Melville went further. In 1578 it was recorded that 'forasmeikle as there is great corruptions in the estate of Bischopes – the Kirk has concludit that no Bischopes shall be electit or made hereafter before the next Generall Assemblie; discharging all ministers and chapters to proceed any wayes to elections of Bischopes in the meanetyme, under the pain of perpetuall deprivations from their offices'.[16] At the following Assembly this was extended 'for all tyme to come', and all bishops already elected were requested to submit themselves to the General Assembly.[17] The pressure of Melville paid off, as is evident from the Second Book of Discipline, sanctioned by the General Assembly – though not by the state – in 1581. Rejecting the supervisory nature of the office of bishop as unscriptural, along with the chapters which created it, Melville and his associates declared that oversight should be in the hands of Church courts, composed of ministers and life appointed elders, consisting of kirk session, presbytery, synod and general assembly, which should cease to be a gathering of the three estates, and be solely that of ministers and elders representing the church courts.

The issue of church government was inextricably linked with that of the relation between church and state. Melville drew a sharp distinction between the two. Following the teaching of Hildebrand, he maintained that the church was above the state. 'There are two kings and two kingdoms in Scotland,' he declared; 'there is Christ Jesus the King, and His kingdom is the Kirk, whose subject King James the Sixth is and of whose kingdom he is not a king, not a lord, nor a head, but a member.'[18] The General Assembly was at pains to point out that 'the power and policie ecclesiasticall is different and distinct in the awin nature from that power and policie quhilk is callit the civill power',[19] and frequently documents of the time record that Christ is the 'onlie spirituall king'.[20] It is little wonder the king complained of 'fiery ministers' who dreamed of democracy, themselves playing the role of *tribuni plebis*.[21] It is little wonder too that James VI increasingly challenged the power and decisions of the General Assembly. In a letter of 1579 to the thirty-ninth General Assembly, read by one of his ministers, John Duncansone, he pointed out that there were some matters which should be left to Parliament, and that decisions of the Assembly should be presented to the estates of the realm.[22] Melville for the moment won the day, largely because, as Smout has observed, his doctrines 'offered a practical solution to certain problems at parish level'.[23]

James was determined to be sovereign in his own realm. To him the Kirk was a state within a state. He demanded the exercise of royal authority over the church, and the legality of the episcopate which would make the bishops willing instruments of the Crown in ecclesiastical affairs. By 1584 James found himself strong enough to achieve his ends by means of the passage of the Black Acts through a servile Parliament, which asserted royal authority in spiritual and temporal affairs, and granted the bishops full Episcopal powers. He contended that it was his intention not to follow the Anglican or Roman pattern, but elevate the dignity of the ministry. James could argue that Melville would make ministers the oracles of God, and as Croft Dickinson has remarked, 'Where lay the need for a king's council, when ministers claimed they were the counsel of God?'[24] Both Melville's theory of church government with its wide chasm between the local congregation and the General Assembly, and his clear distinction between the civil and ecclesiastical paved the way for Rutherford's theory of Divine right of presbytery.

A confrontation between James and the Melvillian party seemed inevitable, and indeed would have taken place if James had not been prepared to compromise. In 1586, it was decided to make bishops moderators of presbyteries, and an Act of 1592 confirmed Presbyterianism. James' flattery of the Church of Scotland as 'the sincerest Kirk in the world', and his insult to the Church of England as 'an evil said Mass in English' came as a shock to both friend and foe. The Melvillian party might have emerged victorious if it had not so strongly objected to James' indulgence of Roman Catholics, and Melville's caustic remark that the king was 'God's sillie vassal'. James seized the opportunity to bring about the fall of Melville and further his own aims. He astutely employed the Act of 1592 to select dates and venues for the General Assembly to suit his own purpose. He so manipulated the Assembly that in 1597 at Dundee a committee of fourteen was appointed to discuss all ecclesiastical matters with the king. Before a year had elapsed, this committee pressed for representation of the Kirk in Parliament, with the result that in March 1598 it was decided that those whom the king appointed as bishops should take their place in the Legislature. The decision was effected in 1600, when royal nominees George Gledstanes, David Lindsay and Peter Marshall were appointed to the sees of St. Andrews, Ross and Caithness respectively, and took their seats in Parliament.

James' accession to the English throne in 1603 greatly strengthened his position. Fond farewells and endearing promises to return to his native soil every third year were offset by the boast that he could rule Scotland with the stroke of a pen from London. With the strength of the Church of England behind him, he had little difficulty in weakening the power of the General Assembly, postponing that of 1604 for a year, and in 1605 postponing it yet further. He hastily and eagerly filled vacant bishoprics with his nominees, and followed up his success in 1606 by summoning Melville and his associates to London, in a vain effort to convert them to Episcopacy. For his criticism of the style of worship he witnessed in the Royal Chapel, Melville was exiled, finding a useful sphere of service in the Huguenot seminary at Sedan. Three of James' bishops were sent to England for consecration, a move which cast doubts upon the validity of the Scottish ordination. Parliament showed its subservience to James by repealing the Annexation Act of 1587, thus restoring temporalities to the bishoprics. The result was, that by 1610 an Episcopal system of church government had been established in Scotland and ratified by Parliament. Although presbyteries still remained in name, power lay with the bishops. With Episcopacy came such practices as kneeling for the sacrament; private administration to the sick; baptism in houses; confirmation and observation of holy days, enunciated in the Articles of Perth, 1618. Under duress the Assembly accepted, but the nation rejected them. Although some ministers were brought before the Court of High Commission for disobedience, it is to the credit of the Scottish bishops that they were not zealous to enforce them. Such was the situation into which Rutherford came when he entered upon his career as a minister of the gospel. For him the challenge could not be refused. Where Melville lay down the sword and the pen, Rutherford took them up.

Parentage and Education

It was in the first year of the seventeenth century that Rutherford first saw the light of day. He was born in the parish of Nisbet, not far from the town of Jedburgh, in Roxburghshire. At that time it was probably a flourishing parish; today, it is no more than a few farms and two rows of cottages. Andrew Bonar, editing Rutherford's *Letters* in 1862, reported that 'there were some old people in the parish who remembered the gable end of the house in which he was born, and which, from respect to his memory, was permitted to stand as long as it could keep together'.[25] Bonar also notes that as late as the 1830s there was a house standing in Nisbet which was identified by an old villager as that where Rutherford was born.[26] Rutherford had a warm spot in his heart for the place of his birth and childhood. Shortly before he died, writing to John Scott, the minister of Nisbet, he expressed the hope that the place to which he owed 'his first breathing', would 'blossem as a rose'.[27]

It is not surprising that, hailing from some of the best farming land in 'auld Scotia', Rutherford sprang from farming stock. There are two somewhat conflicting accounts of his parentage. Wodrow recorded that Rutherford was born of 'mean but honest parents in Teviotdale',[28] but M'Ward, the editor of the first edition of Rutherford's *Letters*, which appeared in 1664, would have us believe he was 'a gentleman by extraction',[29] who used the arms of the Rutherford family. The family is able to trace its descent from a charter granted by David I in 1140,[30] and in the opening decades of the seventeenth century exercised considerable influence in the county of Roxburgh. In 1617 we find a Rutherford, Richard of Littlehaugh, the third son of John Rutherford of Hunthill, acting as Commissioner for the shire.[31] M'Ward, a contemporary of Rutherford, is a fairly reliable informant, although it must be admitted that in planning his preface to *Joshua Redivivus*[32] he stated that his object was to remind the nobility and lairds of their debt to the Covenanting cause, and naturally was tempted to view Rutherford as one of them. On the other hand Wodrow was ever the defender of the poor, and saw Rutherford as their champion. The Rutherfords have been

described as 'an ancient and once powerful border family – of
territorial origin from the lands of Rutherford in the parish of
Maxton, Roxburghshire'.[33]

It may well be that Rutherford was the son of a younger son of
the noble family. His father, after serving as an officer in the Dutch
army, may have inherited part of the family estate and settled as a
farmer in Nisbet (his estate could have been passed on to one of
Samuel's brothers). The fact that the other brother became a
schoolmaster in Kirkcudbright adds further weight to the
impression that Samuel's parents, if not wealthy, were by no means
poor. Thomson's description of Rutherford's father as a
'respectable farmer of moderate circumstances',[34] must be nearer
the mark. Certainly judging from the gravestone inscriptions in
Nisbet cemetery, the Rutherfords were farmers of some substance.
Rutherford frequently complained of persecution, but never of
poverty. Anwoth could not have been a lucrative living: his exile
in Aberdeen and his residence in London during the time of his
attendance at the Westminster Assembly must have been
financially exacting; yet we find him able to employ two doctors
to examine his sick wife. We cannot but believe that Rutherford,
if not wealthy, was a man of means, and came from stock that
enjoyed considerable social status.

Wodrow has preserved a story of Rutherford's childhood, which
is probably no more than a legend. It relates that when four years
of age Rutherford fell into a deep well. On his parents' arrival to
rescue him, they found him sitting on the well safe and sound,
insisting that he had been taken out by the hand of 'a bonnie white
man'. Bonar states that Rutherford had been 'amusing himself
with some companions when he fell in',[35] while Robert Gilmour
maintained that his companion in play was his sister.[36] If we are to
accept Gilmour's version of the story, then Rutherford had a sister
somewhat older than himself.

Young Samuel received his education at Jedburgh. Whether
he travelled daily or boarded in the town we do not know. The
school house was part of the old abbey of Jedburgh, known as
'Latimer's alley'. Because of the national scheme of education
envisaged by the reformer John Knox, many of Scotland's sons

were well educated even though Knox's dream had never been fully realised due to lack of finance. The young Rutherford received sufficient learning and displayed enough talent to enrol as a student in 1617 at Edinburgh's 'Town College', later to become Edinburgh University. Here Rutherford read for a Master of Arts degree.[37]

The College, although hampered by lack of funds, was able to function most effectively, offering a sound liberal education. It followed the mediaeval pattern, four Regents of Philosophy being associated with the Principal in the instruction of students. The Regents administered a tutorial system which resulted in a close liaison between staff and students, especially since they enjoyed personal supervision throughout their college career. The session lasted longer than in modern times, commencing in October and continuing until the following August, some eight to ten hours a day being given to learning. The course over a period of four years was comprehensive, including classics, philosophy and physics. There was a remarkable modernity about educational method in seventeenth-century Edinburgh. Students were not subjected to the laborious and often fruitless business of verbatim recording of lectures. Although there were frequent examinations, much time was spent in discussion between students and professors. These methods must have greatly developed Rutherford's ability to debate, so indispensable to him in later years, especially at the Westminster Assembly of Divines.

Rutherford graduated in the traditional manner at the termination of his four year course. In the evening of the penultimate day, students were required to subscribe to the Confession of Faith before the Principal, and the subject for public debate to be held on the following day was announced. Almost the whole of the final day was spent in discussion, in the presence of members of the College of Justice and other eminent public figures, the evening being reserved for the conferring of degrees by the Principal.

Professor of Humanity
We have no knowledge of Rutherford's activity in the two years which followed his university course, but we may confidently

believe that he was engaged in further study, since in 1623 he was appointed Professor of Humanity. The appointment was made as a result of examination, and in the face of keen competition from three older men, William Hog, David Will and George Hannay. The post to which Rutherford succeeded was instituted in 1597 as a tutorship in Latin. Even when it became a professorial chair it was not so highly rated as the others, the Professor of Humanity not being allocated tutorial groups as other Regents. However, because Latin was the medium of communication in the College, the appointment gradually assumed greater importance, so that by the time of Rutherford's institution it was considered a key post. The examination to which Rutherford was subjected took the form of an interrogation on one of the Odes of Horace, lasting about three quarters of an hour. It is recorded that Rutherford 'after some hesitation was preferred by the judges – because of his eminent ability of mind and virtuous disposition.'[38] Thus Rutherford was elected the sixth Professor of Humanity in the same year as the celebrated John Adamson was made Principal of the College.

Rutherford occupied the Chair of Humanity for two years. It was during this time that he married. His demission of office was in some way connected with his marriage, much to the embarrassment of biographers eager to portray the saintliness of Rutherford. Thomson merely stated that his resignation was the result of 'some indiscretion or irregularity in connection with the formation of this union'.[39] Gilmour also discreetly passes over the matter, employing the words 'some indiscretion connected with his marriage'.[40] Bonar alleges that Rutherford's resignation was brought about by 'a rumour that charged him with some irregularity'.[41] Patently the biographers have made no attempt to discover precisely why Rutherford resigned. Bonar was careful to point out that, no matter how serious the charge against Rutherford, 'no church court took notice of the matter, though these were days when the reins of discipline were not held with a slack hand'.[42] Certainly whatever may have been the nature of the misdemeanour, it is significant that never at any time did his foes resurrect the incident as a weapon to impugn his character.

Crawfurd, who succeeded him as Professor, referred to it merely as 'some scandal'.

What then was the indiscretion? It could well have been that Rutherford married without the Principal's permission, or after his marriage lived out of the College when it was the custom of Regents to live in. One suspects that other sinister forces were militating against Rutherford and that his indiscretion, whatever its nature, provided an excuse for his dismissal from the Chair of Humanity. Investigation shows that it is almost certain that this was so. It is not without significance that Rutherford's demission coincided with the appointment of Rankin as Regent on the 17th November 1625, followed by his installation the following day; indeed the University record makes a specific reference to the coincidence of time, stating that 'Towards the end of November Mr. Rankin the new professor succeeded to Mr. Fairly's charge; about which time, Mr. Samuel Rutherford professor of Humanity having incurred some scandal on account of irregular marriage found it prudent to resign his office'.[43] Rutherford was no friend of Rankin's. They belonged to opposing ecclesiastical camps. Rankin was an ardent advocate of Episcopacy, devoted to Sir John Hay, a favourite of the King and bishops. In 1638, along with fellow Regent, John Brown, he refused to subscribe to the new covenant, composed of the old covenant of 1581 and an enumeration of the various Acts of Parliament in favour of the reformed religion. Dalzel's history of Edinburgh University significantly refers to Rankin and Brown as the 'two obnoxious Regents – persons of whom the greatest part of the nation entertained a most unfavourable opinion'.[44]

It is not really surprising that Rutherford's resignation should coincide with Rankin's appointment. What surprises us is the way in which Rankin became Regent. The Judges responsible for the appointment commended a Mr. Patrick Panter for the post, but the Lord Provost of Edinburgh (David Aikenhead) and the Town Clerk (John Hay) were eager to see Rankin installed as Regent, and used their considerable influence with the Town Council to bring about his appointment, even though the Baillies, Dean of Guild, Treasurer and principle Councillors, who were not browbeaten by Aikenhead and Hay, supported the recommendation of the Judges. Indeed, 'many of the most respectable members of the Council were much offended with the decision, and complained with reason that contrary to the fair mode of proceeding at former elections the opinion of the Judges had not been followed'.[45]

There may well have been a further factor which led to Rutherford's resignation, namely his relations with Principal John Adamson, who was a prominent member of the Court party. If Rutherford's wife, Euphan Hamilton, was the daughter of John Hamilton, the resolute opponent of William Forbes, a close friend of Adamson's, it is understandable that the Principal would seize the opportunity to press for the resignation of the man married to his enemy's daughter. This would account for the strong wording of the Edinburgh Town Council's record: 'For as much as it being declared by the Principal of the College that Mr. Samuel Rutherford, Regent of Humanity, has fallen into fornication with Euphen* Hamilton – has committed a great scandal in the College',[46] a statement which hardly tallies with the University record that Rutherford 'having incurred some scandal on account of an irregular marriage found it prudent to resign his office'.[47] As suggested, it is quite possible that Rutherford did not obtain the permission of the Principal to marry as he should have done – indeed if Adamson was the enemy of Euphan's father, it is unlikely that he would have obtained the Principal's assent for such a union – and the matter was exaggerated by Rutherford's foes to suit their own ends. It is worthy of notice that the Town Council laid the onus for Rutherford's resignation on the Principal, and at the same time saw its way clear to make 'a handsome donation'[48] to Rutherford, which is rather extraordinary if he was known to have been guilty of fornication.

Student of Theology
After resigning his Chair, Rutherford devoted himself to the study of theology. His indiscretion could possibly have preyed upon his mind, bringing about a state of conviction. Frequently in his letters

---

*In the seventeenth century the spelling of names was not fixed. The name of Rutherford's first wife appears variously as Euphan, Euphen and Euphem.

he referred to the inner conflict of soul and perils of youth. To
William Rigg of Athernie he wrote, 'Old challenges now and then
revive, and cast all down. I go halting and sighing, fearing there
be an unseen process yet coming out, and that heavier than I can
answer.'[49] He confessed to a Bethsaida Aird,[50] while an exile in
Aberdeen, that his heart 'was fraughted with challenges', and that
he feared he was an outcast, 'a withered tree in the vineyard, and
but held the sun off the good plants' with his shadow. Most explicit
of all are his words to Earlston the Younger, written in Aberdeen.
'There is not such a glassy, icy, and slippery piece of way betwixt
you and heaven, as Youth,' he wrote. In this particular letter he
referred to 'The old ashes of the sins of my youth' – 'the hot, fiery
lusts and passions of youth'.[51] Was Rutherford reflecting upon his
own bitter experience? It is quite possible that he was. It could
well have been that at this time, like the prodigal son, 'he came to
himself,' experiencing conversion. There is no evidence that before
this period in his life he had any such experience, in fact he
regretted that his conversion was so long delayed. 'I suffered my
sun to be high in the heaven, near afternoon, before I ever took
the gate by the end,' he wrote in one of his letters.[52] We must
however interpret this as something of a literary exaggeration,
considering that he was still a young man in his twenties when he
came to Christ.

Rutherford applied himself to theology with the prospect of
entering the ministry. Care was taken to ensure that candidates
for the ministry were not only well instructed in theology, but
also every endeavour was made to see that they were able
expositors of the Word. Theological students were subjected to a
more rigorous discipline than their fellows. Each Wednesday
afternoon was the occasion for a lecture in theology given by the
Principal. Sunday was a particularly busy day for every student of
theology. He was expected to meet with his Regent at 7 am. Later
came attendance at church, followed by discussion on the subject
of the morning's Bible reading and the sermon delivered.

We can be sure that the man who applied himself with such
energy to Humanity gave himself with equal conscientiousness to
Divinity, and was adequately prepared to administer the Word

and Sacraments on concluding his ministerial training in 1627, when he was licensed as a preacher. While still a student Rutherford earned the reputation of being a gifted preacher of the gospel and a staunch supporter of the Presbyterian cause, at a time when many were becoming accustomed to Episcopacy and its practices. Lord Kenmure, disappointed at his failure to persuade John Livingstone to become minister at Anwoth, offered the charge to Rutherford. A new church was erected for the new ministry, and a new name was added to that succession of worthy ministries which had done so much to keep the torch of Presbyterianism burning brightly in the south west of Scotland.

CHAPTER 2

THE PASTOR

Although at the time of his call to Anwoth, Rutherford had been Professor of Humanity at Edinburgh, and was destined to be both Professor of Divinity and Principal of St. Andrews, as well as one of the Westminster Divines, he is best known to posterity as 'The Good Pastor of Anwoth'. This is all the more surprising, since he was permitted less than a decade to exercise his ministry in one of Scotland's most delightful areas of scenic beauty, backed as it is by the foothills of the Southern Uplands to the north, and facing the Solway Firth to the south. Gilmour described it as 'a veritable Garden of Romance',[1] while Andrew Bonar declared it to be 'the very ideal country church, set down to cherish Godliness'.[2]

Church and manse

Today a traveller could so easily pass by the ruins of Rutherford's church without notice. The sixty foot granite monument, erected in 1842, bears the inscription, 'In admiration of his eminent talents, extensive learning, ardent piety, ministerial faithfulness, and distinguished public labours in the cause of civil and religious liberty.' Although well sited on a hill to the east of Anwoth, it is not easily accessible, and could well be mistaken for just another Covenanter memorial, so common a feature of the landscape in south-west Scotland.

There is nothing to guide one to the scene of Rutherford's ministry but a small post, simply bearing the name 'Anwoth'. The post points along a lane to the ruins of the kirk in which Anwoth's first pastor preached. Today, it is as Thomson described it at the end of the last century, 'an ivy clad ruin',[3] but when Thomas Chalmers visited it in 1826, it was still in use as a place of worship, although a new church was in the process of erection. Chalmers referred to it as 'the identical fabric', and noted datings 1628 and

1633 on some carved seats, coinciding with the period of Rutherford's ministry. With pride Chalmers wrote, 'The pulpit is the same, and I sat in it.'[4] He also made reference to the church bell which he described as 'small', and reported the tradition that formerly it had been a house bell belonging to Lady Kenmure, and gifted to the preacher by the Lady herself.

Thomson bewailed the fact that 'not even a stone' of Rutherford's manse remained, but he was somewhat consoled on discovering there were still those living in his day who could remember it, and were able to offer a detailed description. From information received, Thomson painted the picture of it as 'an old house even in his days built in the baronial style, having belonged to an Anwoth family of rank, and containing more space than the simple pastor needed'. He also tells us that Anwoth folk of the previous generation remembered 'the gigantic hollies which lined the front of the house, while a green field gradually sloped down to the level, along which a tiny burn found its way to the Fleet not far off.'[5] Chalmers wrote that although the house 'had not been used as a manse for a long time', it had been recently occupied. He also described its demolition, which took place only some three weeks before his visit, on August 23rd, 1826, as 'a cruel circumstance', feeling that it should have been spared. So sacred was the spot to Chalmers, he and his company 'mourned over the rubbish of the foundation'. He related that some of the masons, when ordered to demolish it, refused, considering it 'an act of sacrilege', and were 'dismissed from their employment'.

The religious context of Rutherford's ministry at Anwoth
At the Reformation the south-west of Scotland was marked by zeal for the reformed faith. Here in the fourteenth century English Lollards had found refuge. It was a band of Ayrshire lads who first defied the Queen Regent in her attempt to interfere with their preachers. Here too, in Mary's reign, reformers had sought safety. Knox was in the south-west in 1556 and 1562. But for all this there was little to enthuse about spiritually in the south-west as in other parts of Scotland.

The nobility had a vested interest in the Reformation. They

had enriched themselves with church land, but were divided by feuds and jealousies. Their behaviour was characterised by drunkenness, gluttony, profanity, incest and adultery. As long as the local lairds could retain their land and revel in their new-found wealth, they were not interested in the gradual spread of Episcopacy, nor did they oppose the evil of non-residency.* They did not consider Episcopacy as a threat until it was imposed by royal prerogative. Then it was that they saw Presbyterianism as their natural ally. Prior to Rutherford's settlement in Anwoth, when the village was linked ecclesiastically with Kirkmabreck and Kirkdale, the villagers complained that their 'souls were under that miserable extreme famine of the Word', that they had 'only the poor help of one sermon every second Sabbath'.[6]

At the beginning of the seventeenth century, however, there was evidence of growing spiritual awareness. The tide of religious enthusiasm began to flow. Indeed Rutherford's settlement in Anwoth is an indication of the nobility's new attitude towards the Presbyterian minister. Whatever the spiritual situation at the time of Rutherford's advent to Anwoth, a generation before the district had come under the influence of the saintly John Welsh, minister of Kirkcudbright, and son-in-law of Knox. William Dalgleish, who was responsible for the care of the Anwoth folk before Rutherford's arrival, may not have been able to devote as much time to the village as its inhabitants wished, but as Gilmour pointed out, he was a 'resolute adherent to the Presbyterian faith'.[7] We have the testimony of Bonar too, that 'so abundantly blessed were his labours to the people, when he surrendered the charge of Anwoth to Rutherford, upon its being formed into a distinct parochial charge, not only many of the humbler class of parishioners, but the proprietors too, had embraced the doctrine of the Gospel'.[8] With Rutherford's settlement the parishioners had their heart's desire, a minister of their own. During his ministry no one could complain of 'famine'.

The House of Lochinvar, Rutherford's patron at Anwoth, was

---

*non-residency: the practice, common before the Reformation, whereby a priest might live outside his parish and pay someone else to carry out his duties.

one of the families to emerge with a vested interest in the Reformation. Much of the ecclesiastical land held by the Bishop of Galloway and the Abbey of Tongeland had come into its possession. At the time when Rutherford was appointed to Anwoth, the head of the house was Sir John Gordon. He did not enjoy good health, and the administration of his estate was in the hands of the future Viscount Kenmure. Gordon was torn between loyalty to Charles, for the sake of his own preferment, and the desire to establish a strong Presbyterian ministry. Rutherford was naturally encouraged by his patron's zeal for the Presbyterian cause. 'I have good hope that your husband loveth the peace and prosperity of Zion,' Rutherford wrote to Lady Kenmure, 'The peace of God be upon him, for his intended courses anent the establishment of a powerful ministry in this land.'[9]

It was Kenmure's growing fear of Episcopacy, and desire for a powerful Presbyterian ministry, that led him to establish Anwoth as a separate parish in the autumn of 1626, hoping to secure the services of John Livingstone, a thoroughgoing Presbyterian, as the new minister. This in itself is evidence of Kenmure's change of heart. When Cowper, the Bishop of Galloway, had brought about the union of the parishes to please his friends and allies, Kenmure had raised no objections, a failing Rutherford referred to as 'the sins of his father's house'.[10] When Livingstone declined to accept the invitation to take up the work at Anwoth, it was John Kerr, the minister of Prestonpans, who introduced Rutherford as a likely minister for the new parish, so Rutherford informs us in a letter to Marion McNaught.[11] Rutherford was undoubtedly a suitable substitute, being evangelical and a fierce defender of the Presbyterian cause. We cannot date with certainty Rutherford's induction at Anwoth. Probably it was in 1627, judging from the record of a petition of parishioners to the General Assembly of 1638 giving reasons why Rutherford should not be removed from his parish, where it is stated that he had served 'the cuir of Anwoth, these eleven years'.[12]

There is uncertainty, too, as to the manner of Rutherford's induction to Anwoth. Andrew Lamb was Bishop of Galloway at the time. Although a representative of Episcopacy, he was not cast in the mould of Sydserff, the high-handed prelate who succeeded him. Providentially Lamb was a friend of the accommodating Kenmure, and seems to have raised no objection to Rutherford's settlement. Both Bonar and a note in the *Scottish Worthies* based on Wodrow and supported by Rutherford's disciples M'Ward and John Livingstone, affirm that Rutherford's settlement was 'without any acknowledgement or engagement to the Bishop'.[13] This is in keeping with Murray's claim that Bishop Lamb allowed Rutherford to be ordained presbyterially,[14] but it is at variance with the statement that the young minister was required to take an oath of obedience to the Bishop enjoined by a law of 1612.

If there was one principle above all others that Rutherford insisted upon, it was the right of popular election to a parish. When Sydserff attempted to force a minister upon Kirkcudbright, in place of the suspended Glendinning, Rutherford encouraged the Provost of the town to withstand the Bishop's intrusion. 'I would counsel you to write to Edinburgh to some advised lawyers,' he wrote to Marion McNaught, the Provost's wife, 'to understand what your husband, as the head magistrate may do in opposing any intruded minister, and in his carriage towards the new prelate.'[15] To Rutherford any intruded minister was 'a hireling pastor'.[16] Rutherford respected the law, as we learn from his remarks to Marion McNaught,[17] and undoubtedly kept within its bounds, but was ordained presbyterially, since, as Gilmour has stressed, his patron Lord Kenmure 'took a promise from Bishop Lamb that he would not molest Presbyterian ministers or enthral their conscience with Episcopal ceremonies'.[18] It is unlikely that a champion of the Presbyterian cause would allow himself to be shackled by unacceptable ceremonies, even at this early stage.

Preaching

No account of Rutherford's Anwoth days would be complete without some mention of him as a preacher. Although he was called upon to represent the Church and nation at the Westminster Assembly, and was elevated to professorial honour, preaching was his 'first love'. He refused to occupy the Chair of Divinity at St.

Andrews unless he was free to preach. One of his biographers remarked that 'he rejoiced in preaching as the lark or nightingale may be supposed to delight in its song'.[19] In his own day Rutherford was renowned as a preacher, a fame which followed him posthumously into the next century. The existence of copies of his sermons such as that of *Christ dying and drawing sinners to Himself* (originally a series of sermons based on John 12:27-33, preached at Anwoth and re-preached in London, which were printed as early as 1644) and *Tryal and Triumph of Faith* (a revised collection of some Anwoth and St. Andrews sermons printed in the following year, together with forgeries belonging to the following century) witness to the widespread appeal of his preaching.[20]

Exposition for Rutherford meant a careful analysis of a text or passage of Scripture. A typical example is a sermon preached from Song of Solomon 5:7-10, at Anwoth on the afternoon of April 15th, 1647. After a short introduction, he paid considerable attention to the smiting of the watchmen, identifying them as civil rulers, pointing out that in seeking Christ there are persecutions and trouble. In a similar manner the keepers of the walls are identified, and their action in removing the veil is explained. Then follows an exposition of the charge to the daughters of Jerusalem and the instruction, 'Tell Him I am sick of love', explained from the Hebrew as 'weak through love'. Finally, from the words, 'What is thy beloved more than another beloved?' Rutherford becomes rapturous over the glories of Christ.[21]

The Galloway sermons, probably published from notes taken while they were preached, are characterised by short sentences and pointed exhortation, such as, 'Inward grief brings out the spouse's seeking of Christ', and 'Take your pennyworth's of Christ while you have Him'.[22] Frequently too, there is the rhetorical question: 'Are not ministers Christ's stewards?', and 'Shall not hungry bairns get no more nor public allowances in church assemblies?'[23] are but two examples.

His early sermons are frequently punctuated with metaphor, analogy and simile. He refers to 'Christ's pantry'.[24] The congregation is likened to 'hungry bairns',[25] faith is said to be as 'smoke beside fire'.[26] Rutherford loved the homely illustration. There are references to 'dear overseas wares,'[27] 'the empty spoon in the child's mouth',[28] and the 'strait coat for a woman's body'.[29]

Rutherford's earlier sermons are freer, less ordered, more forceful, his later homilies being more doctrinal and dialectic. There is a marked absence of the metaphor and simile, although the homely illustration is still to be found. In his scholarly addresses he employed the language of the schools, with frequent references to original languages and Latin quotations. While there are allusions to contemporary issues, Rutherford did not dwell upon them overmuch; his concern was ever to exalt Christ. He was rapturous over the glories of Christ and the superlative grace of God. 'O what a happiness,' he exclaimed, 'for a soul to lose its excellency in His transcendent glory.'[30] It is therefore understandable that Rutherford had a preference for figurative texts, which readily lent themselves to a Christological interpretation. Wodrow's anecdote of the English merchant who said that the fair little man of Anwoth showed him all the loveliness of Christ, is certainly in keeping with what we learn from Rutherford's sermons.

Rutherford was no mealy-mouthed preacher; wherever there was sin he denounced it. Of the drunkard he said, 'he looks not well upon his lawless lust and desire after drink, and the anger of God that is as hot as fire, and the dishonour of God's name, compares not with his present satisfaction and the roasting of his tongue in hell for ever and ever.'[31] How bitterly he regretted the immorality of his day: 'How many are in the world who live and die in adultery and harlotry, living a profane and godless life, not making conscience of swearing, drinking, breaking the Lord's day and so lose the right way to heaven.'[32]

Rutherford was always at pains to make a point of doctrine clear. Having expounded Luke 15:12, he stated unequivocally, 'The doctrine arising from this is, that it is not against the wisdom of God or the goodness of Christ to permit sinners to fall into sin.'[33] Again in the same sermon, having dealt with the prodigal's return, he stated, 'The doctrine is clear, it is this...' His sermon on the parable of the prodigal son illustrates Rutherford's approach

and method of exposition. He was always careful to identify the
details. In this particular sermon, the father's house is the Church,
the father being Christ: an assertion he goes to great lengths to
support, the two sons representing the elect and the reprobate. He
was not able to resist a thrust at his opponents. For him the Kirk
was the Lord's barn floor, whereon there is both chaff and corn,[34]
the Independents being lampooned as 'those who will have a clean
kirk hereaway'.[35] Rutherford was prone to see a doctrine in every
phrase of scripture. For him the prayer of the prodigal offered an
opportunity to discuss the permissive will of God, and the nature
of sin in God's will. He often answered a question by posing
another. To 'Why did God make man capable of sinning?', he
replied, 'Why does the potter use clay that can so easily be
broken?'[36]

Although, as we have noted, sermons before the Lords and
Commons were more erudite, they were no less biblical and
expository. In these homilies too, there is a zeal to point to the
significance of every detail. In a sermon preached to the Lords on
June 25th 1645 in Westminster Abbey,[37] he did not take up time
with any elaborate introduction, but plunged straight into his
subject, the storm on the Sea of Galilee. He declared that God
was more displeased with the sin of His children than with that of
His enemies. If the suffering of His enemies is painful, how much
more that of His children. Enemies were principally Papists and
Antinomians, the Papists being 'the black devil taking away all
certainty of assurance', the Antinomians being 'a golden white
devil, a spirit of hell clothed with heaven'.[38]

Occasional lapses of grammar may be detected, but more
obvious to the eye and jarring to the ear is the frequent juxta
position of 'this' and 'that' – 'How comes this that men desire to
be away from God' is an example.[39] The reader of Rutherford's
sermons may feel that his partiality for 'but' destroys his felicity
of diction, such as in the sentence, 'But is it but the first sight they
get'.[40] Then too, there is the frequent laboured sentence such as,
'they are set to seek something without God to place their happiness
in, when they may be persuaded they will not get the thing they
would be at';[41] or 'They that love an ill end have a wrong eye

towards the creature that they must have, there is a Providence individually disposing that means shall be furnished to such for attaining their ill end and for giving their unlawful acquisition.'[42]

His supralapsarian* theology in no way blunted the sharpness of his evangelistic appeal or weakened the call for moral effort on the part of his hearers. Divine election was to him a source of immeasurable comfort and strength. Although his sermons were steeped in theology and rich in biblical doctrine, they were geared to the problems of life and punctuated with a wealth of imagery. His most arresting pictures are painted in a sentence. Let three illustrations suffice: 'Pride, lust, laziness and security are the meikle water,' he said, 'the saints are the short legged horse, and down they go.'[43] No doubt he had in mind a Galloway nag floundering in the Solway tide. 'Do not think to buy God's kindness with tears; when the water goes out of the bog, the wind comes in,' he declared.[44] 'Be not like bairns building sandy bourocks at a burnside when presently a speat of water comes and spills all their sport or a shower chases them from their play,' he warned his hearers.[45]

Rutherford appeared upon the stage of history at a time when preaching was being increasingly valued. Preaching as the supreme mark of the prophetic ministry came into its own with the Reformation. It rapidly became a prominent feature of Protestant worship in towns and cities, but did not become common in rural areas until the seventeenth century. Hitherto, what had passed for preaching was nothing more than lengthy recitations of the exploits of saints, with unseemly analogies and crude illustrations, which may possibly explain David Dickson's objection to over-elaboration in sermons. The refusal of the bishops in Rutherford's day to place Presbyterian preachers in parishes strengthened the demand for preaching and stimulated the practice of itinerant preaching, such as that followed by Livingstone and Gillespie,

---

Supralapsarianism is the view, held by some Reformed theologians, that God's decree to save a certain number of sinners logically preceded his decree to permit the Fall. The alternative view, held by other Reformed theologians, reverses the order of these decrees and is termed 'infralapsarianism'.

and for which Blair was brought before the Council.

It is inevitable that Rutherford be compared with his English contemporary John Donne.* Donne's sermons, like those of Rutherford, conform generally to the established pattern, a threefold division and amplification with arguments and illustrations from the Bible, the Fathers and later theologians, concluding with a drawing together into a general or specific application. While Rutherford revelled in the Song of Solomon, Donne delighted to draw upon the vast homiletical resources of the Psalms and Pauline epistles. Donne, perhaps more than any other in seventeenth-century England, made the sermon the highly developed literary art it became, and gave substance to Evelyn's remark that 'The religion of England is preaching', and Charles I's admission that people were governed more by the pulpit than the sword in time of peace.[46] Although Rutherford was a Presbyterian and Donne an Episcopalian, both viewed Rome with grave misgivings. Rome for Donne, as for Rutherford, was the devil's instrument. Donne shared Rutherford's hatred of sectaries. For the English poet and preacher, they were 'not bodies but rotten boughs, gangrened limmes, fragmentary chips, blown off by their own spirit of turbulency, fallen off by the weight of their own pride'.[47] Both Donne and Rutherford have been categorised as mystics, though neither strictly fall into that category.

Great as Donne was as a preacher, there is not the same pre-occupation with the glory of Christ in his sermons as in Rutherford's. During Rutherford's confinement in Aberdeen he wrote, 'I had but one joy out of heaven next to Christ my Lord, and that was to preach Him.'[48] To preach Christ was in his own words 'the apple of my delights'.[49] Few preachers can claim as Rutherford did that they are 'free from the blood of all men'. 'I ceased not,' he wrote to his parishioners, 'while I was among you, in season and out of season, (according to the measure of grace given unto me), to warn and stir up your minds.'[50] 'The fair little man', as Wodrow described him, did not possess the orator's voice,

* John Donne (1572-1631), renowned English poet and preacher, Dean of St Paul's Cathedral, London, from 1621 until his death.

his elocution left something to be desired, his thought was often uncontrolled, nevertheless he was 'one of the moving and affectionate preachers in his time or perhaps in any of the Church'.[51] Gilmour portrayed him as a man 'with two quick eyes which upon entering the pulpit were uplifted to heaven',[52] while the earlier biographer Thomson declared that 'his animation not infrequently grew to rapture'.[53]

Pastoral ministry

Rutherford's biographers record little of his ministry at Anwoth. There was, of course, 'the daily round and common task' which lies to every minister's hand; visitation of the sick, consolation of the bereaved; instruction of the young, and the call to holy living on the part of his parishioners. Thomson painted the picture of him 'wending his way among the ferns and heather, far up among the hills and the haunts of the curlew and plover, crossing swollen streams and dangerous mountain torrents, that he might carry the Divine consolation to some new made widow, and heaven's light to the lowly shieling of one who was ready to die'.[54] The same biographer tells us that 'he was sensitively alive to his own position as one of Christ's undershepherds, appointed to take oversight of souls. He therefore endeavoured to know each individual member of the flock by personal intercourse, and so to place himself in sympathy with each, that if any were afflicted, he was afflicted; and if any rejoiced he rejoiced also. By this means he was the better qualified to adapt his instructions to the spiritual conditions of his people, and the way to their hearts became less difficult when everyone of his parishioners was brought to regard him as a friend.'[55]

Thomson's portrait of Rutherford as the faithful pastor finds confirmation in some words of Livingstone. He wrote that while Rutherford was in Anwoth, 'he was the instrument of much good among a poor ignorant people, many of which he brought to a knowledge and practice of religion.'[56] An assertion by Rutherford's disciple M'Ward that the pastor worked assiduously, 'the whole country being to him and accounting themselves as his peculiar flock', is witnessed by a letter of Rutherford to Marion McNaught, in which he excused his brevity and haste on the grounds that he was 'going about catechising'.[57]

No reader of Rutherford's *Letters* can possibly fail to notice his intense pastoral concern for his flock. On leaving Anwoth in 1636 to serve his sentence of confinement in Aberdeen, he wrote, 'the remembrance of my fair days with Christ in Anwoth and of my dear flock (whose care is my heart's sorrow) is vinegar to my sugared wine'.[58] To another friend on the same day, he wrote sadly of the memory of his flock.[59] Distance did not in any way diminish Rutherford's love for his flock.

The months that followed his banishment from Anwoth brought with them an irrepressible lovesickness and an insatiable longing to return to the scene of his ministry. He solicited the help of Lord Craighall, an eminent lawyer and President of the Court of Session, to intercede with the Bishop of St. Andrews, that he be allowed to return to Anwoth.[60] He requested of his patron, Lord Kenmure, that 'some be dealt with' to effect the resumption of his ministry in the parish.[61] To Rutherford his flock were 'a bereaved people, young ones new-born plucked from the breast'.[62] The pathos of his saddened heart is nowhere more moving than in a letter to Marion McNaught, where he pleaded, 'Pray, pray for my desolate flock; and give them your counsel, when you meet with any of them. It will be my grief to hear that a wolf enter in upon my labours.'[63]

When no longer able to converse with his congregation by reason of his 'exile' in Aberdeen, he sought to pastor them by letter. We can be sure that, just as he pled, counselled and warned them by letter and from the pulpit, he did so in the course of his pastoral visitation. Rutherford was ever eager to win the young for Christ. He had a special interest in the welfare of Grizzel, the daughter of Marion McNaught, a frequent visitor to the manse. He affirmed 'the seed of God is in her, as one born of God', and prayed that 'God's seed would come to God's harvest'.[64] Passionately he wrote to John Gordon of Cardoness, 'I desire your children to seek the Lord. Desire them for me to be requested for Christ's sake; to be blessed and happy and to come to take Christ, and all things with Him.'[65] We find him also counselling Lady

Cardoness concerning the children. His purpose was that they 'seek the Lord in their youth, and give Him the making of their days'.[66]

It was the instruction of both young and unlearned that led Rutherford to compile a catechism. It was in the early years of his ministry that he drafted that which is preserved in the Edinburgh University Library. In a letter to the Elder Cardoness, written after six months of his confinement in Aberdeen,[67] Rutherford referred to the catechism he had taught him. It provides an interesting contrast to the Westminster Shorter Catechism in that it is far less doctrinal, the question itself includes the doctrine, the answer affirming its reason and truth. No doubt Rutherford found this form of catechism more suitable to his rural needs.

Rutherford's *Letters* give evidence of his passion for souls. He implored a certain lady, probably one of his Anwoth parishioners 'to start in time to be after Christ',[68] and he called upon Marion McNaught to take as many to heaven with her as she could, for wrote Rutherford, 'the more ye draw with you, ye shall be the welcomer yourself.'[69] Gracious though he was in appeal, Rutherford could be stern in warning. He came quickly to the point in his letter to the dissolute John Gordon of Rusco. 'I desire you to correct the smaller oaths, swearing, lying, drinking, Sabbath breaking and idle spending of the Lord's Day in absence from the Kirk,' he wrote.[70] Although the Book of Discipline stated that 'great men offending in sick crymes as deserve sackcloath should receive the same in aes weill as the poore', the aristocracy often went unpunished.[71]

In his counselling Rutherford never forgot the temptation he himself faced in his younger days. He viewed youth as a dangerous period in life, 'a glassy age when Satan finds a swept chamber – and a garnished lodging for himself and his train'.[72] He confessed that the 'old ashes' of the sins of youth were at times 'a new fire of sorrow' to him in later days. In a letter to Earlston the Younger he described passion as 'a young green devil, that hath never been buried'.[73] From the depths of his own experience and with tender pastoral concern he wrote to John Gordon the Younger, 'It is not possible for you to know till experience teach you, how dangerous a time youth is – corrupt nature hath a good friend to help youth.'[74]

Rutherford maintained that sanctified thoughts were the only antidote to the lusts of youth, 'green fuel that burn not', and 'water for Satan's coal' as he called them.[75]

Rutherford was as adept in comforting the sorrowing as in counselling the young and warning the reprobate. Not long after taking up his charge in Anwoth he had occasion to write to a mother on the death of her daughter. There is a reasoned tenderness in the words, 'Do you think her lost, when she is but sleeping in the bosom of the Almighty? Think her not absent who is in such a Friend's house. Is the loss to you who is found to Christ?' How evident is his sympathy as he wrote, 'Your daughter was but part of yourself, and therefore nature in you being out and halved will indeed be grieved.' He exhorted the mother to rejoice that when a part of her was on earth, a great part was glorified in heaven.[76] Rutherford sought to console the Viscountess Kenmure on the death of her daughter with the thought that brevity of time means more of eternity. 'If her glass were but a short hour,' he wrote, 'what she wanteth of time that she hath gotten in eternity.'[77] In his own sorrow Rutherford was not unmindful of the trial of others. While *en route* to Aberdeen, he took time in Irvine to write a letter to Robert Cunningham of Holywood in Ireland, who for conscience sake had been deprived of his charge. He reminded his fellow minister that it is 'a more honourable service to suffer for His Name'.[78]

Personal and public life in Anwoth

Rutherford had to endure his own sorrow as well as share that of others. Death robbed him of his two children and disease laid low his wife in the early days of his ministry. For thirteen months she suffered in body and mind before death released her from her pain. He shared this sorrow, as so many other intimacies of life, with Marion McNaught. Writing to her on November 17th, 1629, he reported that his wife was 'sore tormented night and day' and confessed, 'I am so comfortless and so full of heaviness, that I am not able to stand under the burden any longer – my life is bitter to me and I fear the Lord to be my adversary.'[79] The months which followed witnessed a rapid deterioration in her condition, so much so that on February 1st of the following year, he sadly wrote to the same lady, 'My wife's disease increaseth daily, to her great torment and pain night and day – I can hardly believe her disease to be ordinary, for her life is bitter to her; she sleeps none, but cries as a woman travailling in birth.'[80] Rutherford consulted a Dr. Jeally and a John Hamilton in Edinburgh to minister to his wife's condition,[81] but with little hope of recovery. So despairing was Rutherford that he besought the Lord to 'loose her out of her body and take her to rest'.[82] It was indeed with a sense of relief that he informed Lady Kenmure on June 26th of his wife's death.[83]

Apart from his wife's illness and death, Rutherford records little of his family life. For six months after his wife's death his aging mother cared for him, until death too deprived him of her ministry in the manse. He had nine children in all from his two marriages, but we know nothing of them. He makes but a veiled reference to the death of one of them in a letter of consolation to Lady Kenmure on the death of her child.[84] To the distress of his wife's illness, and the sorrow occasioned by the loss of his loved ones, was added the anguish of his own sickness. He complained to Lady Kenmure that he had 'been diseased of a fever tertian for a space of thirteen weeks', and could 'preach but once on the Sabbath with great difficulty' and was not able 'to visit or examine the congregation'.[85] Fortunately for Rutherford when deprived of domestic help and cheer, his dear friends Marion McNaught and her husband sent their daughter Grizzel to be what Thomson described as 'a sunbeam in the house, to light up his desolate home, by her cheerful piety'.[86]

In the autumn of 1629 Lord and Lady Kenmure left the district to reside in England. Not knowing at the time of their departure that they would return within the space of two years, Rutherford feared he might not see them again. 'To my grief,' he wrote, 'I must bid you, it may be forever farewell, in paper, having small assurance ever to see you again – I have received my divers dashes and heavy strokes, since the Lord called me to the ministry, but indeed I esteem your departure from us among the weightiest.'[87]

It is probable that Rutherford feared for Lord Kenmure's faith. His keen pastoral eye and sensitive heart detected the flaws in his

character. Some years later, writing from Aberdeen, he had cause
to rebuke his patron, pleading with him to desist from evil and
turn to Christ.[88] When he was created Viscount Kenmure and Lord
Gordon of Lochinvar by Charles I, he found himself in a most
difficult situation. Devoted as he was to the cause of
Presbyterianism, he suffered such pangs of conscience while
attending the Parliament at which the king was determined to
further Episcopacy, protesting illness he hastened home to
Kenmure castle. He could not rid his mind of the matter, and when
a year later he had cause to revisit Edinburgh the old wound of
conscience was reopened. When Rutherford called on him at
Kenmure Castle, the pastor found his patron plagued by a stricken
conscience and at the point of death. Through Rutherford he found
peace before he died on September 12th, 1634.

Kenmure's repentance and death had a profound effect upon
Rutherford. Later he published a work entitled, *The Last and
Heavenly Speeches and Glorious Departure of John, Viscount
Kenmure*. As a guardian of the church's liberty, Rutherford did
not fail to press home to the nobility the dangers of religious
compromise with princes and parliaments.

It is not surprising that sore trial found him plagued with doubt
at times. It is understandable that in the mists of sorrow and
suffering he should think the Lord his adversary, but faith enabled
him to accept with resignation the crosses he was called upon to
bear. 'I look not to win away to my home without wounds and
blood,' he wrote. 'Welcome, Welcome cross of Christ,' he
exclaimed exultantly, 'if Christ be in it.'[89] It was through his trial
and tribulation that Rutherford came to know the triumph of Christ.
It was in Aberdeen during his period of banishment from Anwoth,
that he gave expression to his philosophy of suffering. 'I am
persuaded,' he wrote, 'that it is the chief errand of our life – that
we might suffer for a time here among our enemies; otherwise He
might have made heaven to wait on us, at our coming out of the
womb, and have carried us home to our country without letting us
set down our feet in this knotty and thorny life.'[90]

Rutherford gave himself assiduously to the work of the ministry
in Anwoth. He was convinced that his presence with his people

was needed. He informed Lady Kenmure that 'he did not stir abroad from the parish'.[91] We get the impression that the early years of his ministry were spent wholly in Anwoth. He complained that his people were like 'a hot iron that cooleth being out of the fire', and that in spite of his efforts 'there was exceeding small fruit of his ministry'.[92]

Rutherford became increasingly the disseminator of political information to the Presbyterians of the district. Then, too, he became manager of burgh elections. He told Marion McNaught that Edinburgh had consulted him to ensure the selection of suitable men from Kirkcudbright, and solicited her help, along with that of her husband, in the rejection of Robert Glendinning and John Ewart, whom he did not think to have the necessary skill and authority. At the end of 1632 or early in 1633 we find Rutherford in Edinburgh, helping Provost Fullarton with this matter. He reported to the Provost's wife that in his appearance before the Council her husband had barely escaped discredit, but had the better of the issue with the Baillies.[93] It appears too that some time later he was in Edinburgh again to deal with some business of his own.

Kindly souls in other parishes not only sought Rutherford's services on special occasions, but coveted his ministry and pressed for his translation from Anwoth. Such calls caused him no little anguish of spirit. In 1634 Rutherford was called upon to take over the spiritual oversight of the neighbouring town of Kirkcudbright in succession to the faithful and saintly Robert Glendinning. Rutherford's letter to Marion McNaught on the occasion of this call is an intimate revelation of the pastor's heart, perplexed as to the Divine will. He wrote 'My soul is under wrestling and seeking direction from our Lord – whither I shall go.' He confessed that there were 'doubtings and fears'. He was anxious to know whether or not he was facing 'temptations and impediments' cast in by God. Sydserff had promised to find a successor to Glendinning, and concerning this there is a touch of irony in Rutherford's words, 'There is cause to thank God for seeing the Bishop hath given you such a promise, he will give you an honest man more willingly than he will permit me to come to you.'[94] Cramond too had high hopes that Rutherford might become their minister, but the future revealed that he was not to preach and pastor but suffer for the Presbyterian cause.

Increasing opposition and banishment

We have seen that during the early years of Rutherford's ministry at Anwoth, he was rarely absent from the parish, his time and strength being devoted to the work of preaching, visiting and catechising. Rutherford, however, soon became a marked man. By 1629, he was widely known as a protagonist of Presbyterianism, backed no doubt by the political power of the Kenmures. A careful study of his letters reveals that increasingly Rutherford was looking beyond Anwoth. On the 17th of November of that year he made reference to a letter from Charles I to John Maxwell, an Edinburgh minister, who later was to become Bishop of Ross. In his letter the king urged the spread of Episcopacy and intimated a celebration of communion in Edinburgh the following Christmas.[95]

Rutherford became Presbyterian counsellor for the south west, receiving information of royalist policy and passing it on to Presbyterian loyalists. In a letter to Marion McNaught, written on June 2nd, 1631, he wrote, 'I have received a letter from Edinburgh informing me that the English service and the organs, the King James Psalms, are to be imposed upon our kirk, and that the bishops are dealing for a General Assembly.'[96]

This particular letter provides a most revealing insight into Rutherford's part in the network of communication among Presbyterians and the fears of his own heart. He made it clear that his task was to communicate such information as he received and referred to confirmation of the facts, but cautioned his correspondent not to pass on the news he had received until he himself had seen her. By this time it is clear that the web of Presbyterian intelligence was well woven, and that men such as Rutherford were greatly disturbed by royalist policy both in England and Scotland. The persecution of the Puritans in England was a distressing omen of things to come in Scotland. Rutherford referred to the imprisonment of the English Puritan Dr. Burton: 'The Lord hath let me see clearly,' he wrote, 'how deep furrows

Arminianism and the followers of it shall draw upon the backs of God's Israel.'[97] It was understandable that Rutherford should become increasingly pessimistic. To Marion McNaught he wrote, 'I have been exceedingly cast down and am fighting against a malicious devil, of whom I can win little ground.'[98] Rutherford found himself drawn deeper into the national controversy from the seclusion of his Galloway parish, so that by 1632 we find him fully committed in the struggle against Episcopacy, a commitment which brought about involvement in the Kirkcudbright elections,[99] and his journey to Edinburgh on Provost Fullarton's behalf,[100] where he helped to marshal the Presbyterian ranks for the expected Parliament.

Far too many ministers were cast in the mould of the cunning Vicar of Bray,* determined at all costs to retain their parishes. As long as the lenient Lamb was Bishop of Galloway, Rutherford could suffer little harm, but his replacement by Sydserff spelled danger for Anwoth's pastor. Many ministers were deprived of their parishes and committed to prison by the Court of High Commission, established in 1610. As early as June 1630 Rutherford saw that trouble was ahead. 'Our prelates,' he wrote to Lady Kenmure 'assure us that for such as will not conform, there is nothing but imprisonment and deprivation.'[101] In that same year, because of accusations made against him by one whom he described as 'a profligate person of his own parish',[102] Rutherford was brought before the Court of High Commission. Archbishop Spottiswoode was prevented from attending, being delayed by a storm at sea. Fortunately for Rutherford, Alexander Colville, one of the judges, stopped the proceedings and the charge was dropped.

Opposition to Rutherford continued, however, so that by 1634 he sensed a coolness towards him in Presbytery. 'I do every Presbytery day see the faces of my brethren smiling upon me, but their tongues convey reproaches and lies of me a hundred miles off and have made me odious to the Bishop of St. Andrews,' he

---

* 'The Vicar of Bray' was a well-known song of unknown authorship, dating from the eighteenth century, about a time-serving cleric who boasts of his accommodating himself to the religious views of kings from Charles II onwards.

wrote.[103] When he expressed his joy at anticipation of the Lord's Supper to be held the first Sunday after Easter in the following year, he feared it would be his last at Anwoth.[104] In 1636 he was accused of treasonable doctrine by adversaries in the Synod. At the beginning of that fateful year we find Rutherford bracing himself for the inevitable conflict he was to face. 'I hang by a thread,' he wrote to the wife of his patron, but rejoiced it was 'of Christ's spinning', there being no quarrel more honest and honourable than to suffer for truth.[105]

Inevitably there soon followed a summons to appear before the Court of High Commission once again, this time at Wigton. Rutherford was charged with nonconformity and deposed from his charge. He was further summoned to appear before the Central Court of High Commission in Edinburgh on July 27th. Rutherford wrote that he was three days before this court,[106] being charged with treason against the king, the ground of which was his *Exercitationes Apologeticae Pro Divina Gratia,** a treatise directed against Arminianism. Treason could not be proved but he was deemed guilty of nonconformity. The proceedings in the Court seemed to have been good natured, but Rutherford complained that he was roughly handled, the Chancellor and others plying him with questions not related to the summons. Although threatened by them, he refused to answer. Lord Lorne boldly defended Rutherford and it appeared the Court would be lenient. The angry Sydserff, eager that Rutherford be found guilty, declared with oaths that he would take the matter to the king, if the judgement of his court at Wigton was not upheld.[107] The Bishop of Galloway was not to be disappointed: Rutherford was deprived of his charge and ordered to be in Aberdeen by August 20th.

---

* 'Apologetic Exercises in Favour of Divine Grace.'

CHAPTER 3

THE PRISONER

Rutherford must have known that his time of suffering would come, as it had come to so many of his colleagues, but he was not unprepared for the cross he was to carry. He wrote to Robert Gordon of Knockbreck, 'Christ hath so handsomely fitted for my shoulders, this rough tree of the cross, as that it hurteth me no ways.'[1] Though heartbroken at the thought of leaving his flock, the pastor rejoiced in anticipation of suffering for his Master: 'I soon go to my King's Palace at Aberdeen, tongue, pen and wit cannot express my joy,'[2] he wrote to Marion M'Naught. When he set out for Aberdeen, determined to be there by the time set for him, he was accompanied by a deputation of his faithful people, arriving in September, 1636. There he resided in a house situated in the Upper Kirkgate.

He travelled by way of Irvine, in Ayrshire, where he enjoyed the luxury of an evening's fellowship with its minister David Dickson. 'What a night that must have been: To hear these two in solemn converse,' exclaimed Bonar.[3] Some time too was spent in Edinburgh, where from his correspondence we judge that he did not receive an unfriendly welcome. 'No face hath gloomed upon me since I left. God's sun and fair weather conveyeth me to my paradise in Aberdeen,'[4] he wrote to his friend Robert Gordon, while to Alexander Gordon of Earlston he was able to report that, 'All men I look in the face, (of whatsoever denomination, nobles, and poor, acquaintance and strangers) are friendly to me.'[5]

Frustration and fears
Aberdeen had been purposely chosen as the city of Rutherford's banishment, not only on account of its distance from Anwoth, but also because of its espousal of the Arminian and Episcopal cause. It is not surprising, therefore, that he met a mixed reception. Not all were unfriendly; Rutherford was happy when he found 'a

lodging in the heart of many strangers'.[6] He rejoiced that some were kind to him, 'many faces having smiled' upon him, but he was forced to admit that 'in the night under their breath others are kind according to their fashion', adding, 'many think me a strange man and my cause not good.' Rutherford was quick to sense a hypocrisy of the city's preachers. 'They pretend great love,' he complained to Lady Kenmure.[7] Nor did it take him long to discover the religious character of the northern city. He saw 'God in few'. 'It consisteth either of Papists or men of Gallio's naughty faith.* It is counted wisdom in the most not to countenance a confined minister,' he declared.[8]

If Rutherford hoped that he would have freedom to preach in the pulpits of the city, then he was bitterly disappointed. The prelates made sure he did not preach in Aberdeen. 'They have added to the rest this gentle cruelty, to discharge me of the pulpits of this town,'[9] he wrote to Lady Kenmure. Nothing frustrated Rutherford more than the ban imposed upon him. In his correspondence there are frequent references to his 'dumb Sabbaths', which burdened his heart and made it bleed.[10] He described them variously as 'festering wounds',[11] 'a stone tied to a bird's feet that wanted not wings,'[12] and 'a great heaviness'.[13] He longed to preach, 'A pulpit would be a high feast for me,'[14] he wrote, and called upon William Gordon of Roberton to pray that he might 'find house room in the Lord's house to speak His Name'.[15] The bitterness of the ban was exacerbated by the memory of happier days in Anwoth. They were to him, 'feast days with the Lord Jesus, now turned into silent Sabbaths'.[16]

Rutherford was greatly concerned for the welfare of his bereaved flock, 'whose care' was 'his heart's sorrow'.[17] In moments of depression he feared that the Lord had 'taken away his crown',[18] in leaving his congregation desolate. This concern was increased by lack of news from his people. 'I complain that Galloway is not kind to me in paper; I have not letters these sixteen weeks but two,' he wrote to Marion McNaught on January 3rd, 1637. There

---

* Gallio (Lucius Junius Gallio) was the Proconsul of Achaia before whom Paul was accused (Acts 18:12-17). He refused to take any view on the Jews' religious concerns. Rutherford is referring here to Arminianism.

is an obvious sense of disappointment too in his words to Robert Gordon of Knockbreck, 'Though all Galloway should have forgotten me, I should have expected a letter from you ere now.'[19] He poured out his complaint also to Lady Kenmure, 'I wish that my friends in Galloway forget me not,' he wrote.[20] To Rutherford it seemed that 'being out of sight was out of mind'. He could not bear to be forgotten by those he loved. 'It may be,' he wrote to Alexander Gordon, 'that I shall be forgotten in the place where the Lord made me the instrument to do some good.'[21]

He was particularly grieved to hear that Sydserff was trying to foist a minister of his own choosing upon the parish of Anwoth. The prelate was so vigorously opposed by the parishioners, however, that he had to give up his plan. 'It shall be my grief to hear that a wolf enter in upon my labours,' Rutherford wrote.[22] Indeed he was so worried about the matter that he begged William Dalgleish, whom he had succeeded at Anwoth, to 'use means to keep my place empty, and to bring me back again to the people to whom I have Christ's right and His Church's lawful calling'.[23]

Knowing well that pressures would be brought to bear upon his pastorless people, and how cunningly prelacy would try to achieve its ends in his former parish, it is not surprising that we find Rutherford writing at length, warning them against practices they should in no way countenance. 'I counsel you,' he wrote, 'to beware of the new strange leaven of men's inventions, besides and against the Word of God, contrary to the oath of this kirk, now coming among you. I instructed you of the superstition and idolatry in the instant of receiving the Lord's Supper, and of crossing in baptism, and of observing men's days, without any warrant of Christ our Perfect Lawgiver. Countenance not the surplice, the attire of the mass-priest, the garment of Baal's priests. The abominable bowing to altars of tree is coming upon you. Hate and keep yourselves from idols. Forbear in any case to hear the reading of the new fatherless service book, full of gross heresies, popish and superstitious errors, without any warrant of Christ, tending to the overthrowing of preaching. You owe no allegiance to the bastard canons, they are unlawful, blasphemies and superstitions. All the ceremonies that lie in Anti-Christ's foul

womb, the wares of the great mother of fornications, the kirk of
Rome, are to be refused.'[24]

Those with strong convictions were fortified by Rutherford's
exhortation, but the banished pastor knew that the weak would
compromise for the sake of their lives and livelihood. Rutherford
found it necessary to write again to his parishioners within the
space of two months, warning them again against Episcopal
innovations. In this further letter he reminded them that at the
Lord's Supper 'they were as banqueters at one table' with the
King. Accordingly they were to 'eat and drink; and divide the
elements, one to another'.* Crossing in baptism he declared to be
'unlawful and against Christ's ordinance'. There was a further
warning against the observance of holy days apart from the
Sabbath. He stressed that the Sabbath was to 'be kept holy and
sanctified with preaching and the public worship of God, for the
memory of Christ's birth, death, resurrection and ascension'. Again
Rutherford expressed his disapproval of anything that savoured
of idolatry, such as the 'worshipping of God before hallowed
creatures, and adoring of Christ by kneeling before bread and
wine'.[25]

There were times when he feared that his ministry in Anwoth
had not laid a strong enough foundation for his people to withstand
the pressures of persecution. He wrote sorrowfully of his 'neglects
when he had a pulpit'.[26] To William Dalgleish he wrote, 'I cannot
tell what is become of my labours among that people, if all that
my Lord hath builded by me be casten down, and the bottom fallen
out of the profession of that parish, and none stand by Christ,
whose love I once preached as clearly and plainly as I could...to
that people, how can I bear it.'[27]

Debates and further threats

It was sorrow enough that Rutherford was barred from preaching
in Aberdeen. He was forced to endure the added sorrow of being
tormented in debate with Dr. Barron, Professor of Divinity since
1625 at Marischal College, who was selected to do verbal battle

---

* The Scottish Presbyterian practice at the Lord's Supper was for church
members to sit around a table and serve each other with the bread and wine.

with Rutherford. We have Rutherford's own word that the debates troubled him. Writing in 1637 to George Gillespie, who in the following year was to become minister of Kirkcaldy, he complained, 'I am here troubled with disputes of the great doctors especially Dr. Barron.'[28] Yet the semi-public debates must have brought some relief to Rutherford, in that he had the opportunity of replying to the accusations made against him from the city's pulpits. He reported to Robert Blair that he was 'openly preached against'.[29] There were several debates; Rutherford wrote to William Dalgleish, 'Dr. Barron hath disputed with me, especially about Arminian controversies and for the ceremonies. Three contests laid him by, and I have not been troubled with him since. Now he hath appointed a dispute before witnesses.'[30]

Because of Rutherford's references to Arminianism, it has been assumed that Barron was an Arminian. Rutherford, however, did not say he was. He wrote that he disputed with Barron 'about' Arminianism, and 'for' the ceremonies. Although Barron was a staunch Episcopalian he was known as an opponent of Arminianism. He and his colleagues in Aberdeen, with the exception of William Forbes, who was created Bishop of Edinburgh in 1634, were most probably moderate Calvinists. The fact was that Barron was an infralapsarian, contending that God having permitted the Fall then decreed the salvation of the elect. This to Rutherford, an ardent exponent of the supralapsarian position, which maintains that predestination takes place before the Fall, was as objectionable as Arminianism.

To Rutherford the whole city theologically was 'corrupt'.[31] It is not surprising that there was a strong possibility as early as 1637 that Rutherford would be transported to some place further north, or even outside the kingdom. 'I find ministers working for my confinement in Caithness and Orkney – because some people here (willing to be edified) resort to me,' he confided to John Stuart, the Provost of Ayr;[32] while to Alexander Gordon he wrote, 'Banishment out of the kingdom is determined against me, as I hear this land is not able to bear me.'[33]

Indeed in 1637 the prospect of Rutherford ever exercising a ministry in Scotland seemed very remote, so much so that he

considered ministering abroad, should he be released from his
confinement in Aberdeen. Many English Puritans had found refuge
in New England. Rutherford, in a letter to John Stuart, the Provost
of Ayr, named it as a possible retreat,[34] but friends thought that he
would be more profitably employed on the continent. Robert
Baillie was eager that he should obtain a post in Utrecht, Groningen
or Rotterdam.[35]

Rutherford, however, still clung to the hope of being restored
to Anwoth, even when the prospect seemed most remote. In a
letter to Lady Kenmure he expressed his longing for deliverance,
and wrote that he hoped his friends in Galloway would effectually
act to this end.[36] He penned the same sentiment in a letter to Marion
McNaught: 'I would that honest and lawful means were essayed
for bringing me home to my charge. It concerneth you of Galloway
most, to use supplications and addresses for this purpose, and try
if by fair means I can be brought back again. As for liberty, without
I be restored to my flock, it is little to me, for my silence is my
greatest prison.'[37]

It appears that his pleas for help did not go unanswered, judging
from his words to the same correspondent in 1637. Even in
Aberdeen there were those willing to support an appeal for his
release. 'Many here,' he wrote to Marion McNaught, 'rejoice now
to pen a supplication to the Council, for bringing me home to my
place and for repairing other wrongs done in the country.'[38]
Rutherford called upon Mrs. Fullarton to procure signatures of
three or four hundred noblemen, gentlemen countrymen and
citizens, hoping that so weighty an appeal would frighten the
bishop with no fear of reprisals against the appellants.[39]

Freedom from confinement
Rutherford was forced to wait for his freedom until radical religious
and political changes took place. By 1638 the greater part of
Scotland was seething with unrest, and ready for rebellion. The
Canons and the Book of Common Prayer* had become
increasingly obnoxious to Presbyterians in Scotland, as to the

---

* The Book of Canons and the Book of Common Prayer were imposed on
the Church of Scotland by Charles I. The Book of Canons (1636) directed

Puritans in England. As Gilmour pointed out, it was not merely their content that aroused the anger of the Scots, but also the arbitrary way in which they were imposed, 'without the consent of the national church'.[40] Whether or not Jenny Geddes hurled her stool at the head of the prelate who attempted to read the collect for the day from the hated prayer book on that fateful Sunday, July 23rd, in St. Giles Cathedral, an incident sparked off what Scottish historians have delighted to call the 'Second Reformation'. The signing of the Covenant in Greyfriars Kirkyard, Edinburgh, on March 1st, 1638, showed clearly that Scotland was ready to throw off the yoke of religious bondage. As Godfrey Davies has pointed out, 'Patriotism and Protestantism combined in resistance.'[41] Throughout the land the solemn Covenant was read and signed in kirks amid scenes of great rejoicing.

Although the Covenant became a cause of bitter sectarian strife, and the obstacle preventing any agreement between Charles and Scotland, in 1638 it brought a unity of all classes in Scotland. Signatories to it bound themselves to oppose Stuart religious impositions, which were said to be unwarranted by the Word of God, contrary to the Reformation and to Acts of Parliament, and tending to the re-establishment of popery and tyranny. King Charles was given the opportunity to recognise the strength and determination of Scottish feeling, but he was too blind and obstinate to bow before the storm. He was determined to be obeyed at all costs.

Although the Covenant promised to uphold the sovereign, the Scots were forced to call a General Assembly to redress their grievances. It met in November and at Parliament in the following May. The presence of laymen in the General Assembly representing the presbyteries was of great annoyance to Charles. In spite of the High Commissioner's efforts to dissolve the Assembly, it resolutely continued its work, rejecting Canons and Service Book, abolishing the Court of High Commission, establishing a Presbyterian system of church government, and

the organisation of the church. The Book of Common Prayer (nicknamed 'Laud's Liturgy' after the Archbishop of Canterbury) set out the form of service to be used in the church.

deposing fourteen bishops who absented themselves from the Assembly. The Archbishop of St. Andrews admitted that all which prelacy had built up over three decades was destroyed in a day. Rutherford could be confined no longer; joyfully he returned to Anwoth, which he described as 'that little vineyard of the Lord's planting in Galloway'.[42]

Activities and anxieties in Aberdeen

Although Rutherford's voice was silent during the period of his confinement in Aberdeen, apart from the public debates, his pen was never more active. It is to this period of his life that we owe so many of his letters, indeed the majority of them (two hundred and twenty out of three hundred and sixty-five which have been preserved for us). Through the ministry of the pen he comforted and challenged. We find him writing to a lady on the death of her husband, comforting her with the exhortation, that 'seeing he walked with the Lord in his life, and desired that Christ should be magnified in him at his death, she ought to be silent and satisfied'.[43] We find him counselling the young, warning them to beware of the sins of youth and rejoicing to hear of those who in their early days had come to Christ.[44] Who was more fitted to encourage the Provost of Kirkcudbright in his opposition to the Bishop of Galloway than one who was banished because he refused to accept the pretensions of prelacy? Earnestly he desired him 'to give honour and authority to Christ and for Christ; and be not dismayed for flesh and blood.'[45] Who could have written with greater feeling, 'Grace groweth best in the winter',[46] than Rutherford? Who was more able to encourage the oppressed than one who exclaimed, 'Oh what I owe to the file, to the hammer, to the furnace of my Lord Jesus'?[47] 'Till ye be in heaven,' he wrote to John Fergushill, the minister at Ochiltree, 'it will be but foul weather; one flower up and another down. The lintel-stone and pillars of the New Jerusalem suffer more knocks of God's hammer and tool than the common side wall stones.'[48] Rutherford discovered in Aberdeen that 'suffering for Christ is the very element wherein Christ's love liveth'.[49]

Removed from the busy pastoral life of Anwoth, Rutherford suffered much in Aberdeen from what he called 'upbraidings';

seasons when his sensitive soul and tender conscience were tormented by over-introspection. This led to spiritual depression, amounting to almost self-despair. In such times he did not regard suffering as a garland of which to be proud, but rather a grief which lay heavily upon his heart. Even so he was not prepared to exchange his 'weeping in prison for the Fourteen Prelates' laughter'.[50] He still claimed that his Lord's cross was 'overgilded and oiled with comforts'.[51]

Rutherford, like so many others, discovered the fickleness of the human heart in the harrowing experience of confinement. A voice within cried out against God. He confessed, 'I like a fool summoned my husband and Lord and libelled unkindness against Him.'[52] It seemed to Rutherford that he had 'a rumbling and a raging devil',[53] which exploited the corruption of his nature to the full. He complained of the 'old challenges', which revived in him. 'I go halting and fighting, fearing there be an unseen process yet coming out and that heavier than I can answer.'[54] He described his unregenerate nature as, 'that idol, that whorish creature', 'the master idol we all bow to'.[55] He feared like Paul that he would become 'an outcast – a withered tree in a vineyard'.[56] Thankfully he recognised the Lord's hand in the searchings to which his soul was subjected, and acknowledged that his 'apprehensions were with child of faithless fears and unbelief.'[57]

Confinement in Aberdeen, however, was not all sorrow for Rutherford. There he experienced seasons of spiritual ecstasy. He witnessed that he was never closer to the Lord than in his period of confinement. This conviction was never stronger than in the February and March after his arrival in the city. On February 16th he affirmed that Christ had led him up to a point in Christianity he was never at before, and that 'all before was but childhood and bairns play',[58] while four days later he rejoiced that he had reached such a point in Christian experience, he thought little of former things.[59] On March 4th, writing to David Dickson[60] and Robert Douglas[61], he shared with them his new-found intimacy with the Lord. For Rutherford, Aberdeen was both shadow and sunshine. 'Except I have some cloudy days,' he wrote to a fellow minister, 'for the most part I have a king's life in Aberdeen'.[62]

CHAPTER 4

THE REFORMER

Rutherford's enforced exile in Aberdeen came to an end sometime in February 1638[1] (the exact date being unknown[2]). He was informed that the Privy Council had received a declinature* against the Court of High Commission. He did not return to his beloved Anwoth, however, until the July of that year. In June, on the eve of Hamilton's arrival,* we find him preaching to the nobility, commissioners and townsfolk in the college hall at Edinburgh. In this particular sermon he vehemently condemned ceremonies and bishops, incurring the displeasure of Hamilton for his attack on the episcopate. When Rutherford arrived in Anwoth, his rural parish must have been a welcome sight to him after years of exile in the city of Aberdeen, and the excitement of revolution in a capital feverishly preparing for armed resistance to Charles Stuart. James Reid, the nineteenth-century chronicler, informs us that 'Divine Providence having mercifully restored him to his flock in the year 1638, he again laboured with great diligence among them. Many persons attended his ministry from all quarters in that neighbourhood'.[3]

Brief return to Anwoth

Rutherford was not allowed to enjoy the rural peace of the Solway for long. Scotland at that critical hour had need of him. On November 21st, along with his fellow ministers Dalgleish and McLelland, together with the elders Earlston, Knockbreck and

---

* In Scottish law, a declinature is a refusal to acknowledge the jurisdiction of a court.

* James, 3rd Marquis (later 1st Duke) of Hamilton, was Charles I's Commissioner in Scotland. In the king's view, the General Assembly of the Church of Scotland could not meet lawfully without Hamilton's permission and presence.

Glendinning, he was chosen to sit in the Assembly of December, 1638.[4] This Assembly debated the validity of elders' commission, Hamilton, supported by Strang, Principal of Glasgow University, questioning the right of those delegates appointed by votes of elders. A committee of four, which included Rutherford, was appointed by the Assembly to confer with Strang on the matter.[5]

Another committee of the Assembly was of the opinion that Rutherford's talents were wasted in the obscurity of his Kirkcudbrightshire parish, and that the cause of Presbyterianism would be better served by his translation to one of the country's centres of learning. Edinburgh cast its longing eyes upon him; even Aberdeen, the city of his exile, pressed for him; but St. Andrews was successful in obtaining his appointment to the Chair of Theology at St. Mary's College. Howie, the Principal, although an Episcopalian, was retained along with two other Episcopalian members of staff.

The Assembly of 1638, having cleared Rutherford of the charge against him, declaring the sentencing court to have been illegal, employed him in committees for the investigation of ceremonies and the planting of churches, and committed to him the task of examining the charge of Arminianism brought against a James Affleck.[6]

Parishioners, local lairds and clergy throughout Galloway, along with neighbouring presbyteries, protested strongly at Rutherford's removal from Anwoth. Rutherford himself, although concerned for the welfare of the national church, was saddened at the decision of the Assembly to remove him from Anwoth. 'My removal from my flock is so heavy to me that it maketh my life a burden to me; I never had such a longing to death,' he confessed to Lady Kenmure.[7] During the period of his banishment his folk had remained faithful to him, refusing to accept a successor of Sydserff's choice. Rutherford objected that the Commission had no right to translate him without receiving objections from congregation and presbytery. When he learned that the Assembly had sustained the decision of the Commission, Rutherford determined that there would be no more 'silent sabbaths', consenting to take up his new appointment only on condition that he be associated in the ministry of the Word with the town's minister, Robert Blair.

St. Andrews

After taking up residence at St. Andrews in December 1639, Rutherford was busily engaged in academic and administrative work, the latter being occasioned by Principal Howie's mismanagement of the College, a fault which led to his resignation. It is therefore understandable that he exercised little influence on the Assembly of 1640, which in that year was held in Aberdeen, to emphasise the triumph of Presbyterianism. It was an Assembly, however, which sadly revealed the divisions in the Presbyterian ranks.

The divisive issue was the convening of 'private meetings', a custom derived from Huguenot practice, and introduced into Scotland from Ireland. Zachary Boyd* had been largely responsible for the revival of the custom in Scotland, being arraigned before a court for the holding of them. Blair and Livingstone, who had both ministered in Ireland, were familiar with them, while Rutherford adopted and encouraged the practice, defending their legality by treatise. Baillie, however, viewed them with concern, interpreting any form of extremism as the thin edge of Brownism*, or Independency. The issue had come to a head in Stirling, where the Laird of Leckie was brought to task by his minister, Henry Guthrie. At the Aberdeen Assembly, Guthrie appealed to the north-east for support in his criticism of the Laird.

A committee was appointed which included Rutherford, but was strongly biased in favour of Guthrie. Rutherford strongly defended the practice of holding 'private meetings', but in the cause of unity agreed to withdraw his opposition to an Act forbidding the practice. The issue, however, was raised again at the St. Andrews Assembly in 1641, where Leckie, not content to let the matter rest, was determined to indict Guthrie.

---

* Zachary Boyd (1589-1653), minister of the Barony, Glasgow.

* 'Brownism' was a name often applied to Independency (Congregationalism). Robert Browne (c.1550-1633) was a Puritan separatist who founded a number of independent congregations in England.

'Private meetings' continued to be a matter of contention throughout 1643, even though the Assembly of that year did its utmost to silence it, in view of the presence of English delegates. Guthrie insisted upon the re-imposition of the Aberdeen enactment. Henderson maintained that this was unnecessary, decisions on the matter being left to the wisdom of synods and presbyteries. The trouble was that the Aberdeen Act was open to diverse interpretations, so much so that in 1647 it was deemed necessary to pass a further Act.

Other issues which divided Presbyterians at the Aberdeen Assembly were the practice of kneeling in the pulpit and the recitation of the 'Gloria', matters which clearly called for the compilation of a Directory of Worship.

Unfortunately we know little of Rutherford's academic work in St. Andrews. All that has been preserved are some students' notes of his lectures on the subjects of 'Revelation' and 'The Canon of Scripture' given in Latin. It is to Rutherford's credit that, although now elevated to high office, and enjoying the sunshine of national approval, he did not forget his brethren who were suffering for conscience sake, such as Alexander Leighton in England, and those he addressed as 'Prisoners of Christ at Dublin'. To Leighton he wrote, 'Oh who can suffer enough for such a Lord, and who can lay out in bank, enough of pain, shame, losses, and tortures to receive in again the free interest of eternal glory.'[8] To the oppressed in Ireland he sent a message of hope; addressing them as 'prisoners of hope', he bade them open their windows and look out by faith, and 'behold heaven's post, (that speedy and swift salvation of God)' that was coming to them.[9]

While Rutherford lectured in St. Andrews, momentous events were taking place in the kingdom. Charles Stuart's determination to suppress the Scottish rebellion by force was thwarted by the Scots victories at Dunslaw and Newburn.* The King, too, was harassed by the Long Parliament in England, determined upon not only the redress of their grievances, but also the introduction of a Presbyterian polity throughout Britain. Parliament decided that a Confession of Faith and Catechism should be drawn up by

---

* The so-called First and Second Bishops' Wars in 1639 and 1640.

delegates from both sides of the border. It was fitting that Rutherford, so long a champion of the Presbyterian cause, should be chosen as one of the Scottish delegation.[10]

Episcopacy
The Reformation settlement in Scotland had been in jeopardy from the beginning of the seventeenth century. James, intent upon imposing Episcopacy, restored civil privileges to the bishops. In 1610 two courts of High Commission were established to strengthen the cause of Episcopacy. Further, the Articles of Perth in 1618 legalised and popularised such practices as kneeling at communion and private administration of the sacraments, as well as the observance of Christmas and Easter. By the time that Rutherford commenced his ministry at Anwoth in 1627, Episcopal practices were common in many parts of Scotland. Charles I was more determined than his father that the Church of Scotland should be Episcopal. A letter from him in 1629 urged conformity to Episcopal practices, and announced that communion would be celebrated in Edinburgh that Christmas.

To the Presbyterian Scots this was a terrible omen of impending troubles. It is not surprising that frequently Rutherford referred to what he regretfully called 'the present state of this decaying Kirk'.[11] He lamented the persecution of faithful pastors and professors; the intrusion of those he called 'bastard porters'; rulers prostituting the cause of religion for the sake of policy, and the 'multitude ready to receive easy religion – enjoined by authority'. So serious did the situation seem to the Presbyterians that a covenant of prayer was made to preserve the Presbyterian heritage; the first two Sundays in February and the intervening six days between the first and second Sundays of every quarter being devoted to intercession.[12]

Rutherford could not remain silent, and he was soon in the forefront of the battle. 'I dare not for my soul be silent, to see my Lord's house burning and not cry, "Fire, fire", ' he wrote to Marion McNaught.[13] He was greatly disturbed by news in a letter from Edinburgh, that there was to be a Synod of Bishops or General Assembly. He was so afraid that at this Synod commissioners would be chosen by the Bishops, he could not apply himself to his studies.

There is reference in Rutherford's correspondence as early as November 17th, 1629, to the imposition of the English Liturgy.[14] We have reason, therefore, to believe that its introduction went on apace some years before Laud's elevation to the archepiscopal see of Canterbury in 1633. A letter dated June 2nd, 1631, makes reference to the subject, as a result of fresh news from Edinburgh. Rutherford expressed deep concern that 'the English service, and the organs, and King James' Psalms'[15] were to be imposed upon the Kirk.

By this time the Bishops had been successful in settling many of their own nominees in the parishes, and the innovations were widely accepted. Indeed Rutherford found himself facing opposition in his own locality, and complained that he was 'most unkindly handled by the presbytery'.[16] Rutherford foresaw a bitter conflict. He wrote to Marion McNaught of his 'great heaviness'[17] over the state of the Kirk, and called upon John Kennedy, a Baillie of Ayr, to 'pray continually, and wrestle, for the life of a dying breathless kirk'.[18] He predicted to Lady Kenmure that there would be 'ere long a fiery trial upon the Church',[19] the Lord intending 'to melt and try the land'.[20]

To the Calvinists of Scotland the root of the trouble was the spread of Arminianism.[21] Rutherford bewailed 'the deep furrows' its protagonists made 'upon the backs of God's Israel'.[22] To the seventeenth century Scot, Arminianism went hand in hand with prelacy. Of it was born the hated service book, complied by James Wedderburn, Bishop of Dunblane, John Maxwell, Bishop of Ross, with the assistance of Sydserff and Ballenden, Bishop of Aberdeen. After its compilation in Scotland it was submitted to Laud and Wren, the Bishop of Norwich, for revision. Such changes as were made by the revisers appeared to be in a popish direction to the Scots.

Its use was enjoined by the Privy Council on the 20th December, 1636, and proclaimed at the Cross of Edinburgh the following day, but it was not published until the end of 1637. Rutherford, referring to its imposition in a letter to the Provost of Ayr, declared that it was ordained 'by open proclamation and the sound of a trumpet to be read in all kirks of the Kingdom'.[23] Its imposition aroused the anger of the Scottish Presbyterians, not only because they believed it to be alien to their Reformation ethos and foisted upon them without consultation, but also because it was said to approximate more to the Roman Missal than the English Book of Common Prayer.

The new 'fatherless service book' was an anathema to Rutherford. As we have seen, it drew forth strongly worded letters of warning to his parishioners in Anwoth, at the time of his confinement in Aberdeen.

Read prayers were abhorrent to Rutherford. 'I could never see precept, promise, or practice for them in God's Word,' he wrote. 'I never had faith to think well of them. In my weak judgement it were good if they were out of the service of God. I cannot think them a fruit or effect of the Spirit of adoption.'[24] Rutherford opposed them too, because they were contrary to Presbyterian practice. 'Our church never allowed them, but men took them up at their own choice,' he maintained. It was enough for them that 'the saints never used them, and God never commended them'. Prayer, for Rutherford, was 'a pouring out of the soul to God'.

Other equally obnoxious practices for Rutherford, as we have seen in the letters to his parishioners, were kneeling and the wearing of the surplice.[25] His objections arose out of his conception of the Christian ministry. God's servant was in no way a priest or mediator between God and His people. He opposed any form of Episcopal ordination, which in his view gave rise to a priestly concept of the ministry. In objecting to kneeling at communion Rutherford was not in any way detracting from the dignity and sanctity of the Christian ministry, rather he believed that he was maintaining its scriptural nature. He saw the danger of materialism, which can so easily lapse into idolatry, as Paul expressed it, 'the worship of the creature rather than the Creator'.[26] 'Kneeling,' he declared, 'when used as a religious service is the external adoration of that bread, in presence of which we bow as before the delegated representative of God, be our intention what it may.'[27] To Rutherford, kneeling before a consecrated creature, standing in the room of Christ, was the very essence of idolatry.[28] 'Worshipping of God before hallowed creatures, and the adoring of Christ by kneeling before bread and wine should neither be permitted within the walls of Anwoth's kirk, nor practised by the people in any other place,' he wrote to his parishioners.[29]

Rutherford's invective against vestments, such as the surplice, is couched in what may seem strange language to the twentieth century reader. For him, as for the Puritans in England, the surplice savoured of Romanism. He objected to the Articles of Perth, partly because of the assertion that the King had power to enjoin the wearing of the surplice, as well as 'other mass apparel'.[30] There was no doubt in his mind that the surplice was 'the attire of the mass priest'.[31] Equally repulsive to Rutherford was the sign of the cross in baptism, and the observance of Feast days, even Christmas and Easter.[32]

Rutherford never made any secret of his objections to the Canons. They were the work of Sydserff, Maxwell, Ballenden and Whiteford. Having been drawn up they were submitted to Laud and two other English prelates for revision, becoming law in 1635. Not only were they objectionable because of their imposition by royal authority, they were also opposed because of the unrestricted powers they gave to Bishops, and the ceremonial rites enjoined, especially in connection with the administration of baptism and the celebration of the Lord's Supper. Rutherford admitted it was because of his opposition to these canons that Sydserff was particularly angry with him.[33]

Scottish Presbyterianism owed more to Calvin than Luther. Luther, for all his reforming zeal, was not prepared to make such a decisive break with Rome as his fellow reformer in Geneva. Lutheranism continued to embrace Episcopacy. It is not surprising, therefore, that the news of a meeting of prelates to consider reconciliation between the Scottish Kirk and the Lutherans should cause grave concern. The very possibility of reconciliation witnesses to the spread of Episcopacy in Scotland. The fact that it was sponsored by the professors of Aberdeen University, (such a stronghold of Episcopacy and the city of Rutherford's exile), led the banished pastor to suspect that 'a reconciliation with Popery' was intended.[34]

Westminster

Rutherford could not have been overlooked in the selection of
eminent men to represent the interests of the Scottish Kirk at the
Westminster Assembly of Divines. He confessed that he was highly
honoured by this appointment, but at the same time affirmed that
his 'faith was never prouder than to be a common rough country
barrowman at Anwoth'.[35] Rutherford's contribution to the
proceedings was well acknowledged. Baillie, one of his fellow
commissioners, declared that 'Mr. Samuel for the great parts God
hath given him, and special acquaintance with the question in hand,
is very necessary to be here'.[36] This testimony was confirmed in a
letter from the Synod of Divines at the close of the Assembly's
proceedings, on the occasion of Rutherford's return to Scotland.
'We cannot but restore with ample testimony of his learning,
godliness, faithfulness and diligence', wrote Adoniram Byfield,
the scribe, at the order of his colleagues.[37]

Although there was no fear of persecution as there had been
hitherto, the task of the Westminster Assembly was by no means
easy. The very constitution of the gathering posed a problem. There
was disagreement between Lords and Commons as to the wording
of the document that gave it existence, and Charles I not
surprisingly refused his assent to its meeting.

The proceedings of the Assembly were protracted over a period
of six years. The issues were too complex, and the theological
atmosphere too emotive, to bring about a speedy solution to the
religious problems of the united kingdoms. Because of the length
of the proceedings, the Scottish Commissioners were allowed to
return to Scotland by rota to report progress to the Kirk Assembly.
Rutherford, however, accompanied by his second wife, Jean
McMath, whom he had married in April 1640, four months after
his arrival in St. Andrews, and the two children of this marriage,
did not quit until the task was completed. Alas, London brought
well-nigh as much sorrow to Rutherford as Anwoth. He returned
to his native country in 1647, bereft of his bairns.

Prolonged residence in the English capital did not prove
attractive to the Scots. 'It is so grievous to us to be so long tyme
detained here,' he complained to the General Assembly. 'We do

heartily desire a faire doore to be opened for our returne,'[38] they
wrote. When after three and a half years of deliberation the
Confession of Faith and Catechism were not formulated, it is little
wonder the Scottish Commissioners reported, 'we very judge that
these things will take a long tyme, we are so weary with our
exceeding long absence from our particular charges, that we
humblie entreat from you a permission to return, so soon as you
may think fitt.'[39] Their plea was only partly successful, the
Assembly thinking it fit to retain the services of Rutherford and
Gillespie in London. The Lord Chancellor, Lord Warriston and
Robert Baillie took their leave of London on December 25th, 1646,
and the Earl of Lauderdale on the 12th January in the following
year.[40]

In spite of the common heritage of Puritanism and resistance
to Charles I's ecclesiastical policy, there were major differences
of opinion in the Assembly. Puritanism produced a great variety
of thought and as yet the principle of toleration was accepted only
by a few, and in practice it did not extend to prelatists and papists.
Having been summoned by Parliament the Westminster Assembly
was Erastian, and the Scots encouraged it to challenge its sponsor.
Clarendon spoke contemptuously of its membership, but it must
be noted that five of its members became bishops during his period
of political office. Carruthers, in his account of the Assembly,
points out that sixty-five of the delegates were under the age of
forty-five; fifty-nine above that age, and only seven over sixty-
five, so that it could hardly be criticised as an assembly of the
senile.[41]

Nor was it an assembly of the unlettered. One hundred and
twenty-six were university men, thirty-four were BD's; twenty-
three were DD's; and fifty-two held Fellowships. Arrowsmith and
Harris were famous for their Latin scholarship; Coleman, Lightfoot
and Gataker were Hebraists, while John Harris was also a Professor
of Greek. Thirty had published books. The pulpit was represented
by Goodwin, Marshall and Palmer. Rutherford and Twisse were
theologians of international repute, while Wallis, later to become
Professor of Geometry at Oxford, was a mathematician of renown.
The smallest though most vociferous party were the

Independents led by Nye. Goodwin belonged to them, and so did Bridge, the scholar. Simpson, also of their number, was deemed to be a pastor with the reputation of a preacher.[42] Baillie[43] cites Joseph Caryl, William Carter, John Philips and Peter Sterry as being Independents, but they were not so opposed to Presbyterianism as their fellows, and given certain concessions would have been quite happy with a Presbyterian system of church government. Anthony Burgess and William Greenhill gave only occasional support to Independency. Even Nye, a stalwart for the cause, was willing to accept the parish of Kimbolton, and Goodwin, the Presidency of Magdalene College.

Although the leading Independents were anti-erastian they had moved considerably from the position of the Brownists in Elizabeth's reign. They now occupied a position somewhere between Browne and Johnson*. They were prepared to accept an executive eldership in church government, providing that the elders were responsible to the congregation. Their independency, however, prevented them from accepting association of churches, except for mutual consideration and help, a principle which was diametrically opposed to Rutherford's insistence upon the Divine Right of Presbytery.

These Independents could justifiably contend that they were more united than the Presbyterians, who were divided into three schools, Calamy representing a distinct Presbyterianism; Marshall favouring the Scottish system, while Wallis had a love for the old liturgy.

Although there were only two Erastian divines, they must be classed as a third party. Of these two, Thomas Coleman, minister at Blyton in Lincolnshire, was thoroughly Erastian; the other was John Lightfoot, who sometimes supported Coleman. Both, as Rabbinical scholars, were profoundly influenced by the system of government established in Old Testament Israel, often referred to at that time as the 'Jewish Church'. Among the lay members

---

* Francis Johnson, expelled in 1589 from his Fellowship at Christ's College, Cambridge, and imprisoned for expressing Puritan views. After pastoring among Independents on the Continent, he returned to England and was imprisoned in 1593 for his separatist convictions.

who supported the Erastian cause were Selden, Whitelocke and
St. John. The Erastians could usually count on the support of
Parliament.[44]

The Scottish commissioners, Henderson, Baillie, Rutherford
and Gillespie, were assisted by lay commissioners, Johnston, Lords
Maitland, Argyll, Loudon and Balmerino, who took up their duties
later, and occasionally spoke in the debates. Neither Robert
Douglas nor the Earl of Cassillis ever attended, while Maitland
and Johnston were rarely absent. The Scots did not consider
themselves an integral part of the Assembly, refusing to sit as
such, maintaining that they were the commissioners of a national
church. Further, they were commissioners to Parliament, so that
they occupied a privileged position. The Scots had the right to
initiate debate and veto decisions, as well as hasten them.

All four Scottish Divines were distinguished men. Henderson,
according to Hetherington, was 'the most eminent',[45] his learning
being extensive. Gillespie was an able debater, far too able for
Selden, Lightfoot and Coleman. Baillie rarely engaged in debate,
but his sagacity was valuable in deliberation. Rutherford had
gained the reputation of being an able controversialist long before
going to Westminster. His qualities of heart and mind made him
an expert in debate. His intense spirituality, coupled with clarity
of intellect and warmth of feeling, made him a most worthy
opponent of the Independents, yet made him 'at the same time,
love and esteem' those who held to Independency.[46] His syllogistic
style of reasoning proved to be particularly effective in debate.

The need for Scottish military help in 1643-4 strengthened the
arm of the Scottish commissioners at Westminster. The
Independents resented the degree of influence the Scots exerted
through the Grand Committee*, and did their utmost to counter it.
The Grand Committee maintained that it was a corporate body;
Cromwell's action on September 13th, 1644, compelling the Grand
Committee to revise 'differences in opinion of the members of
the Assembly in point of Church government', weakened the

---

* The Grand Committee, consisting of representatives from Parliament and
the Westminster Assembly and the Scottish commissioners, was set up to
administer the terms of the alliance with Scotland.

power of the Scots. A sub-committee of seven was appointed without any Scottish commissioners being included. The privilege of final revision which the Scots had hitherto enjoyed was denied them, the Independents insisting that proposals should go directly to the House. The Scots were reduced to the level of single units in the Grand Committee. The Scottish Commissioners retaliated by contending successfully that no report of the Grand Committee should be concluded until it had first been passed by the Assembly, and thereafter forwarded to the Commons.

The Assembly was divided into three committees. Reports formulated by the committees were referred back to the Assembly. The Prolocutor, Dr. Twisse of Newbury, presided, assisted by two assessors, Dr. Cornelius Burgess and Mr. Herbert Palmer. When Twisse died, Herle took his place, and on the death of Palmer, Gouge became an assessor. These were assisted by two scribes. Members of the Assembly were required to take an oath not to maintain anything except that which they believed in sincerity and in truth. No resolution was made to any question on the day it was proposed. The Commons in vain tried to discourage long speeches, but brevity was well-nigh impossible, when every statement had to be supported by reference to scripture. Rutherford was one who complained of delay caused by the length of debates.[47]

Although the debates were lengthy, the work was carried out thoroughly. Debates on Holy Scripture, God's eternal decree, Christ as mediator, Christian liberty and the power of the civil magistrate proved to be the lengthiest. Most of the chapters took three or four days to present. It was deemed necessary to appoint a revising committee on July 8th, 1646. This committee carried out its work until December 8th, 1646, when a larger advisory committee was appointed. By September 25th, 1646, it was possible to send up the first nineteen chapters to the Commons, and by November 26th the Confession was completed, only a few minor amendments needing to be made before its presentation to the Commons on December 4th, and to the Lords on December 7th.

That was not the end of the Confession story however, since on October 9th the Commons had demanded the inclusion of proof texts. The work of supplying these began on January 6th, 1647. A small committee was responsible for selecting them chapter by chapter, the work being completed by April 5th. A further ten days work was required to carry out revision, then they were added to the Confession and presented to both Houses on April 27th, 1647. The Confession was speedily adopted in Scotland, where three hundred copies were printed for the use of the General Assembly. It was sanctioned by the Scottish Assembly on February 7th, 1649.

The Confession was a triumph for the Scottish supralapsarian school of theology. The debate on the 'Eternal Decree', comprising the third chapter, was particularly intense. Debate began on August 29th over the title, it being eventually decided to accept the simple title 'Of God's Eternal Decree'. In the debate, somewhat surprisingly, Rutherford took a position which was slightly less rigid than his customary supralapsarian one, but it was this view which triumphed. In the debate the Amyraldian view* of the atonement was rejected. Rutherford claimed that to make all men salvable was to make all men justifiable. Even the most moderate form of Amyraldianism seemed to him to be the thin edge of the wedge of Arminianism.

Under pressure from the Scottish Parliament on October 12th, 1643, authority was given to the Westminster Assembly to draw up 'a Discipline and Government...agreeable to God's Holy Word...and nearer agreement with the Church of Scotland'. The debate began on October 12th with a speech by Seaman on the nature and work of church officers. Three committees were appointed to consider the matter on October 17th.[48] On October 19th the second and third committees reported, but debate as to the names and number of these officers continued until October 27th, when the first committee reported its conclusions. Then followed the debate on the report. It commenced on November 2nd, with a consideration of the office of pastor.[49] Baillie informs

---

* The view of Moïse Amyraut (1596-1644), French Protestant pastor and theologian at Saumur. He held that Christ died in a (hypothetical) universal sense for all humanity, but in a particular sense only for the elect, to whom God grants saving faith. Consequently it is sometimes called 'hypothetical universalism'.

us that the Scots took no part in the debate, since according to 'a paper given in by our brethren before we came...the Assembly did debate and agree anent the duty of pastors.'[50] The only point of contention in the debate was the issue as to whether the public reading of the scripture was the duty of the pastor.[51] Marshall strongly contended that the reading of the scripture was not an ecclesiastical office, it was the exposition that made it so. Palmer objected to this argument, taking the opposite view. Rutherford, following Henderson's *Government and Order*, 1641, made clear his position in his *Peaceable Plea.* 'We acknowledge no reading pastors,' he wrote, 'but only pastors gifted, who are able to cut the word aright.'[52] The final decision was that reading belonged to the pastor's office, a conclusion which, by including probationers, was acceptable to the Scots. Other pastoral duties such as admission to the sacrament, catechising and visiting the sick were resolved with little debate.

The divisive issue was the form which a national system of church government should take. At this point Independents stood opposed to Presbyterians. Since Rutherford had suffered so much for the Presbyterian cause, it was understandable he should champion it in the Council of Westminster, resisting the introduction of any ecclesiastical polity which was likely to threaten its existence. Parliament was predominantly Presbyterian in its sympathies, while the Army under Cromwell was disposed to favour Independency. At the outset of the struggle with Charles from 1640 to 1642, power lay with Parliament, but with the war it inevitably shifted to the Army. Although Rutherford acknowledged the saintliness of the Independents as 'those of all that differ from us, came nearest to walkers with God',[53] he saw in Independency a dangerous rival to Presbyterianism. The Scottish commissioners reported to the General Assembly that there was 'nothing more pernicious, both to church and state, than the leaving of all men to an autonomy in religion'.[54] So numerous did the sects in London appear to Rutherford – Anabaptists, Libertines, Seekers, etc. – and so obnoxious were they to him, that he doubted whether there were many sound ministers in the capital.[55] He condemned the Libertines as 'fleshly, abominable antinomians'.[56] He objected to the Seekers on the ground that they rejected the sacraments of the Church. It was the ecclesiastical confusion in London that prompted him to write *The Divine Right of Church Government* which was published in 1646. He penned his *Survey of the Spiritual Anti-Christ* to counter Antinomianism, and the polemic entitled *A Free Disputation against pretended liberty of conscience* to expose the dangers of Independency. The two latter works were published in 1648 and 1649 respectively, after his return to Scotland.

English Presbyterianism was almost as suspect to the Scots as Independency. When they arrived in London in 1643, Baillie wrote 'As yet a Presbytery to this people is considered to be a strange monster.'[57] English Presbyterianism was by no means as rigid as that of the Scots. While the Commons in 1642 were determined to uproot Episcopacy, the Westminster Assembly gave hope to those who favoured a form of primitive Episcopacy. The roots of English Presbyterianism can be traced to Geneva through Thomas Cartwright.* Scottish Presbyterianism owed much to the French model. Calvin advised English Presbyterianism to submit in non-essentials to the state. Consequently English Presbyterianism was to some extent Erastian. That is probably why it failed as a national system of church government. English Presbyterianism placed little emphasis on the place of the kirk session, and was opposed to the concept of the ruling elder. To English Presbyterians the elder was either pastor or one who advised and assisted him. It could very easily become either a form of Episcopacy on the one hand, or federated Congregationalism on the other.

Clearly the Scots had much to do if they were to convert the Westminster Assembly to their thoroughgoing brand of Presbyterianism. Scotland was determined to obtain a uniformity of ecclesiastical government in the British Isles, as Henderson announced in the General Assembly of 1641. When the Commons spoke of 'such government as may be most agreeable to God's Holy Word', the Scots interpreted that as Scottish Presbyterianism and none else. Where the English envisaged a civil league with the Scots, the latter were determined upon a religious union.

---

* Thomas Cartwright (c.1535-1603) was the most influential Presbyterian theologian among the Puritans of the Elizabethan period.

Although the English were not prepared to go as far as the Scots demanded, there were many English ministers, who, so vague as to the real nature of Presbyterianism, wrote to the Scots for information. The reply came from Henderson, mainly taking the form of a warning against Independency.

The Scots saw their form of Presbyterianism as a panacea for the ills of the nation. During the course of the Westminster Assembly, the General Assembly of the Church of Scotland addressed several letters to Westminster, requesting a speedy conclusion of its business, to which it received no reply. On November 8th, a reply drafted by Tuckney and Marshall was considered by the Commons and taken by Burgess to the Lords, but it did not meet with approval, the Lords desiring that it contain nothing but courtesies and civilities to the General Assembly.[58] The delay in establishing a sound Presbyterian polity in Britain was seen by the Scots as the root cause of the nation's misery. Rutherford was particularly eloquent concerning what he referred to as 'the sins of the land'.[59] On 15th September 1647, he moved in vain for a general fast in the Assembly. He bewailed the fact that 'it was not yet time to build up the house of the Lord',[60] because many in church and state were too indifferent. A peaceable and brotherly way had been suggested but had been deserted, Rutherford complained.[61]

In the discussion on church government the Scots postulated four permanent officers: pastors, teachers (doctors), ruling elders and deacons, government being the prerogative of the first three. They further advocated a fourfold system of church courts: session, presbytery, synod and national assembly. Marshall reported from the Grand Committee to the Assembly on the Scottish paper. He declared that it had not been debated by the Committee, and referred it to the Assembly. The Assembly proceeded to debate it until November 21st. Independents maintained that pastor and doctor were two different offices in substance, a contention that in the main was supported by the Scots, although they were not prepared to distinguish the offices completely. The Assembly as a whole disagreed.

It was in the ruling elder debate, when the very essence of

Scottish Presbyterianism was being questioned, that Rutherford's voice was first heard, supported by a formidable list of names such as Drs. Temple and Smith; Messrs Vines, Price, Hall, Lightfoot, Coleman and Palmer. When Henderson had strongly advocated the function of the ruling elder, pointing out that the ruling elder existed in many reformed churches and had been found 'very prosperous in the Church of Scotland', Rutherford followed with an exegesis of 1 Timothy 5:17. In a debate in which Rutherford particularly distinguished himself, he found himself opposed by the moderate Presbyterians led by Gataker, who viewed with concern the intrusion of laymen into spiritual affairs. In this the moderate Presbyterians were joined by such Independents as Nye and Bridge.[62]

It was in his defence of Scottish Presbyterianism that Rutherford was most eloquent. Henderson for all his qualities was not at ease in a metaphysical atmosphere. Rutherford was able to provide the scriptural, patristic and doctrinal proof demanded by the Assembly. On April 16th, in a most convincing speech, Rutherford contended that the church at Ephesus indicated a Presbyterian structure. He maintained that so many visible saints living in one city were but one church in regard to church government.

Rutherford was especially eager to guard against any curtailment of the power of censure in government of congregations. In this he enjoyed the support of Henderson, faced as he was with opposition from some English Presbyterians, who set themselves against any power of censure and denied the right of congregational eldership.[63] Rutherford also cited the case of the Jerusalem church, as against Burrowes, stating that 'Presbytery doth not rule constantly as a particular eldership but occasionally'.[64] By 26th February, 1644, the Assembly was prepared to accept that 'the church at Jerusalem consisted of more congregations than one',[65] and by the 28th of the month it was agreed there was also diversity of language. The Assembly went further, accepting that the several congregations were under one presbytery. Rutherford contended that the apostles preached and baptised, not as apostles but as elders. 'Why,' he asked, 'shall we not say that they did govern as elders?'[66] He was opposed by Goodwin, who argued that Acts 15:1

by no means proved that believers in Jerusalem constituted one church, forming one presbytery. In the debate on March 13th, Dr. Gouge, referring to Acts 15, maintained that a standing presbytery is indicated in verse 4a and a synod in verse 6. In reply the Independents argued that the decree was extended to all churches throughout the world, over which the elders in Jerusalem had no control. Rutherford asserted the Presbyterian polity by contending that (1) doctrinal power is in the hands of elders, not of single teachers, (2) doctrinal power and that of jurisdiction in an assembly are the same, (3) a rebuke given by a synod juridical differs only in degree from excommunication.

Rutherford was insistent upon maintaining the judicial powers of the church. On January 31st, 1644, in the process of the excommunication debate, he voiced his objections to the phrase 'impenitently persisted in', insisting upon the inclusion of the phrase, 'when sufficiently convinced of them', arguing that, 'in matters of doctrine it is a hard thing to convince that the erronious person is convinced in his own conscience'.[67] On October 20th, Coleman made reference to *Divine Right of Church Government and Excommunication*, objecting to the excommunicated being classed by Rutherford as heathens and publicans. Rutherford defended his assertion, contending that there was no contradiction between being admonished as a brother, and being a heathen and publican.[68]

The Presbyterial principle was also at stake in the ordination debates. A preliminary debate on the subject arose in the discussion on the power of the apostles, in which Rutherford took some part. On January 26th Parliament requested speed in view of the pressing need for pastors. On March 19th, following an appeal by the Earl of Manchester to supply ordinands for Cambridge and other places, the Assembly considered laying aside doctrinal issues and concentrating upon pastoral problems, but the Independents strongly objected, fearing that this was the thin end of the Presbyterian wedge. Consequently the proposal was abandoned on February 2nd until the weightier matter of presbytery was settled. In these debates it was alleged that men like Apollos (1 Cor. 3:5) were ordinands without congregations. Calamy strongly objected to this assertion, citing Rutherford that 'ordination is like setting a stone in the ring'.[69] Rutherford took a prominent part in the discussion, arguing in favour of ordination before election, thus distinguishing carefully between them.[70] He believed that the power of ordination rested with the whole Presbytery, not merely with preaching elders.[71] Rutherford as a Presbyterian objected to the congregation's right to ordain, expressing his objection to the Assembly on May 8th.

Rutherford is probably best remembered for his insistence upon a congregation's right to choose its pastor. During the ordination debate of 18th March, 1644, he declared, 'The Scriptures constantly give the choice of the pastor to the people. The act of electing is in the people; and the regularising and correcting of their choice is in the Presbytery.'[72] This was the principle for which the seceders fought at the time of the disruption in 1843. They took their stand upon the Assembly's decision that 'no man shall be ordained minister of a particular congregation, if they can show any just cause of exception against him'.[73] Thus intrusion was rejected by the Westminster Assembly.

Rutherford also took a leading part in the compilation of the catechism. His experience as a pastor at Anwoth was invaluable. A variety of catechisms was available in England, while in Scotland those of Calvin and Craig were widely used, but by 1630 the supply of those was limited. Rutherford was forced to compile his own. When the committee for the Directory of Public Worship was appointed, Herbert Palmer, who had himself compiled a catechism, was entrusted with the task of compiling a catechism for the Assembly.

The proceedings began with the presentation of Palmer's compilation, but it proved to be unacceptable. The Scots saw this as an opportunity to supply a catechism of their own design. Rutherford's catechism as it stood was too natively Scottish to appeal to the Westminster Assembly, although the catechism presented may well have been the work of Rutherford. The report of Palmer's committee was given on May 13th, 1645. It contained an outline catechism, but owing to prolonged wrangling, by December 1646 only a quarter of Palmer's catechism had been accepted.[74] So involved and complicated did the issue of the catechism become that by January 14th, 1647, it was decided to produce two catechisms, a shorter and a larger.

The Scots took little part in the subsequent work on the catechisms. By this time Henderson was dead, and Baillie had returned to Scotland before their compilation began. Gillespie left London in May, 1647, when the work of the larger catechism was underway, and Rutherford set off for his native land before the shorter catechism was finally presented. The larger catechism was completed on October 15th 1647; the shorter just over a month later, being presented to Parliament on October 25th, the proofs of both given to the House on April 14th, 1648.

It has been generally assumed that Henderson was the leading figure among the Scots at Westminster, the other commissioners being relegated to the role of assistants. Certainly Henderson was leader of the team, but the Scottish commissioners were very much a team. Rutherford's and Gillespie's voices were heard more often than that of Henderson in debate. The Scottish delegation would have been extremely weak in debate without Rutherford. He not only brought his convincing power of argument to the Assembly, he also brought with him a wide experience of church life and a well-stocked theological mind. Rutherford appeared as the champion of Presbyterianism.

CHAPTER 5

THE APOLOGIST

Any record of Rutherford's life would not be complete without some reference to his writings. Indeed he was more powerful with the pen than in the pulpit. During his lifetime some sixteen works were published, and six posthumously.[1] A study of these works enables us to see Rutherford as theologian, Presbyterian protagonist, political philosopher, and correspondent.

The theologian

Rutherford may not be considered a great theologian, nor may it be claimed that he was an outstanding exegete, although he possessed the qualities that are essential in a good exegete – alacrity of intellect, familiarity with ancient languages and adeptness for illustration. He had the ability to systematise rather than expound theology. He left behind him a theology which endured for the two centuries which followed. His fame spread not only throughout Britain but to the Continent as well, especially Holland, as his invitation to professorial chairs in Harderwyck (1648) and Utrecht (1651) testify. Rutherford was regarded as the chief protagonist of the Calvinist cause in its conflict with Arminianism, following as he did lines laid down earlier by William Twisse.

The qualities which earned Rutherford a reputation as theologian are clearly shown in three Latin works, *Exercitationes Apologeticae pro Divina Gratia* (1636), *Disputatio Scholastica de Divina Providentia* (1650) and *Examen Arminianismi*, published posthumously by Nethenus, 1668, in Utrecht. In the first of this triad of theological works Rutherford displayed his ability to debate. Before penning this particular work, Rutherford read two of Twisse's productions, *Dr. Jackson's Vanity*, published in 1631, a criticism of the Dean of Peterborough's discourse on Arminianism, and *Vindiciae Gratiae Potestatis ac Providentiae Dei*, published in 1632, a folio of five hundred pages. Twisse passed to Rutherford the ultra Calvinism of England, which in turn he popularised in Scotland. Rutherford's *Disputatio* is lecture material delivered to students at St. Mary's which appears to have been carefully prepared for publication. It is mainly concerned with divine will in relation to human sin, being very metaphysical in character. It is a work which probably more than any other reveals Rutherford's breadth of learning, quoting as he does from the Fathers to the Reformers, Augustine, Bradwardine and Twisse being supreme.

Examen Arminianismi is a work of very high standard. As the title indicates, it is an examination of Arminianism, an orderly statement of Rutherford's own theological beliefs. The manuscript was taken to Holland by Rutherford's scribe M'Ward, who handed it over to Nethenus for his perusal. Nethenus, with the help of Robert Trail, one of Rutherford's students, revised the manuscript, checking it carefully with students' notes, possibly those of Trail himself. The revision took the form of an erasion of extraneous material along with the omission of digressions concerning sectaries and a reconsideration of chapter headings. Nethenus added a preface to the work. In *Examen Arminianismi* Rutherford expounded his supralapsarian position, formulated by such Dutch theologians as Voetius, Essenius and Nethenus.*

In 1655 Rutherford published *The Covenant of Life Opened*, followed soon after by *Influences of the Life of Grace*. Both belong to his closing years and were consequently penned in the context of the Protestor controversy.* Rutherford appears to have sought refuge from its rancour by turning his attention to a consideration of the grace of God. *The Covenant of Life Opened* is a popular exposition of grace. By the multiplicity of quotations from Calvin,

---

* Gisbert Voetius (1589-1676) was Professor of Theology at Utrecht and had a major influence on the development of Reformed piety and practical theology.

Matthias Nethenus (1618-1686) was also a professor at Utrecht and a supporter of Voetius in theological controversies in the Netherlands.

Andreas Essenius (1618-1677) was a student of Voetius and a professor at Utrecht.

* For the conflict between Protesters and Resolutioners, see chapter 6.

Rutherford revealed his dependence on the Genevan reformer.

In *Influences of the Life of Grace*, which was published in London, 1659, Rutherford stressed the power of irresistible grace in the life of a believer. It is a work written in full prose, which, although couched in technical terminology, reflects Rutherford's spiritual pilgrimage.

The English work *Christ Dying and Drawing Sinners to Himself* was originally sermons preached from John 12:27-33, probably during his residence in London. In 1647 he collected these sermons into a homiletic treatise, adding a paper entitled *Sundry digressions of the Times* which contained excursions into every field of current controversy.

A further work, *The Power and Prevalency of Faith and Prayer*, wrongly called by Bonar, *The Power and Prevalency of Truth and Prayer*,[2] is based on Matthew 9:27-31. It was discovered by J. D. Ogilvie and published in Edinburgh in 1713, with an introduction by Allan Logan. Along with it, printed for the first time, was *A Testimony left by Mr. Rutherford to the work of the Reformation in Britain and Ireland before his death with some of his last words*. The first reference to this testimony is to be found in John Currie's *Essay on Separation*.* William Wilson, in his *Defence of Reformation Principles* (1739), contended that it was not the work of Rutherford, but this contention is unacceptable. Not only is the *Testimony* in Rutherford's style and language, the manuscript was received from a granddaughter of Rutherford and the latter part of it is to be found in M'Ward's *Joshua Redivivus*.

Although Rutherford quoted widely in his works, scripture, providentially preserved, was his supreme authority.[3] He maintained that revelation through scripture was necessary because of human imperfection and ignorance of God. It is to scripture we must turn, Rutherford contended, for the formulation of fundamental doctrine, and for him Old and New Testaments were equally and verbally inspired. In his *Examen* he discussed the relation between the Word and the Spirit. Rutherford rejected both the mysticism of George Fox, with its theory of the 'Inner Light'

---

* John Currie (1679?-1765) was minister at Kinglassie and engaged in controversy with the Seceders who left the Church of Scotland in 1733.

and the rationalism of Episcopius,* who denied the necessity of supernatural light for understanding, '*sentire et judicare de verbo Dei est peccatum.*'[4]

In his doctrine of God Rutherford voiced the orthodoxy of his age. It was Calvinistic in thought, although he differed in emphasis from Calvin. Unlike Calvin his approach was speculative, rather than dogmatic. Rutherford, in his zeal to maintain the unity of the Godhead, regarded Vorstius and later Arminians as tri-theists.[5] The foundation of all theology of the Godhead for Rutherford was belief in the absolute freedom of the divine will. God, he argued, could not be bound even by the necessity of His own nature; God not being without law, but not bound by law.

While Rutherford denied freedom to men, he accorded it to God.[6] This exposed him to the criticism that his God was an oriental despot. God's motive, according to Rutherford, was His declarative glory, creation declaring His power, wrath and justice; redemption revealing His love. This made creation little more than a Divine caprice, grace alone preventing Him from being a despot. God, he declared, does 'What He pleaseth, holily and wisely and most freely'.[7]

While Rutherford emphasised the transcendence of God, he did not reject the doctrine of immanence. Immanence to him was not the mechanical operation of divine power through inherent laws. There was no place in his scheme of thinking for chance or impulse. He even went so far as to maintain that God was concerned in the sinful acts of men, escaping from his dilemma by arguing that the concurrence was physical not moral.[8] Rutherford sought to avoid the supralapsarian tendency which made God the author of sin. Such a position was repugnant to him. Accordingly he adopted the traditional Augustinian concept of sin as moral disintegration resulting from conflict of the human will with the divine.

To understand Rutherford's doctrine of sin aright, we need to

---

* 'Episcopius' was the assumed name of Simon Bischop (1583-1643), an Arminian theologian condemned by the Synod of Dort in 1619. This Synod of the Dutch Reformed Church affirmed the Calvinistic understanding of salvation in opposition to the Arminian views of the 'Remonstrants'.

notice his concept of the 'Fall'. Here he parted company with traditional Calvinism in that he maintained that concupiscence, not pride, was the prime cause of Adam's sin. For Rutherford, Adam before the 'Fall' was neither mortal nor immortal, death and immortality being the consequences of sin. After the 'Fall' all men came under the condemnation of God. Man had a blind instinct to search for God, but no power to find Him. Arminius, on the contrary, credited fallen man with the ability to believe, along with power to do good or evil, but human will required supernatural assistance to operate for good. Rutherford argued that if man by his own willpower could lay hold on God, then grace was unnecessary.

Arminians contended that the supernatural power which assisted the human will was prevenient grace, an aspect of that common grace which God made available to all after the entry of sin into the world, a doctrine repudiated at the Synod of Dort. This concept of common grace was totally unacceptable to Rutherford.[9] He equally rejected the teaching that grace is mediated before conversion in answer to prayer, on the grounds that no fallen man would pray for such grace. The most that any man can do before conversion is to make external preparations for change of heart and life.

Grace, for Rutherford, was a special irresistible gift belonging exclusively to the elect, imparted by the Spirit; not passive acceptance but active co-operation, by putting oneself in the way of receiving it.[10] For Arminius and Episcopius it was no more than moral persuasion, which could be resisted by human will. Rutherford gives the impression that he denied free will to men under grace, as well as before conversion, although in his *Influences* he credits the converted will with good. 'Though there be no merit,' he wrote, 'in diligent seeking and hearing the preached gospel, it is good to be near the fountain for all that.'[11]

Seventeenth-century Calvinism was disturbed by the pronouncements of the Dutch Remonstrance of 1610, which, while asserting election, savoured strongly of Arminianism by proclaiming that Christ died for all. Rutherford maintained that Christ died only for the elect,[12] a contention much at variance with the teaching of Richard Baxter* and Amyraut. 'God has no intention to save all,' Rutherford wrote in the *Covenant*, 'Though He says all that believe shall be saved, nor comes such an offer from Christ's intention to die for all and everyone.'[13]

At the beginning of the seventeenth century the Scottish doctrine of election was *infralapsarian*, predestination was held to have taken place after the 'Fall'. Rutherford had no hesitation in rejecting theories of election voiced in the Westminster Assembly. He was a supralapsarian, maintaining that there was but one decree, as opposed to the infralapsarianism of moderate Calvinism which multiplied the divine decrees. Rutherford's theological position arose from his doctrine of divine will. What God foresaw, He willed. This meant that election could not possibly be conditional upon faith,[14] faith being the consequence not the cause of election. A doctrine of general election embracing all who will believe was rejected by Rutherford.[15] For him, in opposition to the Arminians, election was an act of God which takes place in eternity. Rutherford went so far as to assert that election did not even result from the merits of Christ, since election is not to grace but to glory, election preceding the believer's appropriation of Christ's merits.[16]

Rutherford's doctrine of election may seem stern and extreme to all but ultra Calvinists, but it appears even sterner when we examine his view of reprobation. According to Rutherford, as election precedes creation, so does rejection. He argued that sin is not the cause of rejection and in any case God is not compelled to justify His rejection of the reprobate. Divine rejection is an act of inscrutable wisdom. God is under no obligation to justify Himself to His creature. Rutherford attempted to stop short, though not very successfully it would appear, from holding God responsible for man's sin, by stating that reprobation was a denial of grace. There is a hard fatalism in Rutherford's doctrines of predestination

---

* Richard Baxter (1615-91), Anglican curate of Kidderminster, held the view that Christ died for all men, a view shared with Moïse Amyraut of Saumur. Baxter also held that for justification, the righteousness of Christ imputed to believers must be complemented by their evangelical righteousness.

and election, an extremism which goes so far as to maintain that not only are the numbers of the elect and reprobate decided, but also their very acts, '*Quia absolute decrevit omnes actus contingentes ut probatum est.*'[17]

With regard to covenants Rutherford followed the popular line of distinguishing between a covenant of works and that of grace. A threefold division is discernible however in Rutherford, brought about by a subdivision of the latter. In the Adamic covenant he saw a promise of eternal life conditional upon obedience, but any rights man may have possessed under the covenant were forfeited through sin, and thereafter he was dependent upon the free grace of God.[18] In his treatment of the doctrine of grace Rutherford distinguished between a covenant between God and Christ, and a covenant of reconciliation between God and man in Christ. Christ as Mediator, he maintained, was in no way inferior to the Father, indeed 'the sufficiency of Christ's death depends upon the infiniteness of His person'.[19] In his explanation of the covenant of reconciliation, Rutherford found himself faced with the problem of the 'whosoever' of the gospel. To escape from his dilemma he fell back on the old argument that while the appeal is universal, only the elect will believe; divine justice decrees it.

The assertion of the Synod of Dort that Christ's death is *sufficienter pro omnibus* was not only ridiculous to Rutherford, it was also dangerous. Christ died only for the elect, according to Rutherford, the reprobate not even enjoying any of the blessings which result from Christ's death.[20] Rutherford the theologian appears to be at variance with Rutherford the preacher. No homilist or author could speak or write more fervently about grace than Rutherford. Grace in his heart embraced those whom his theological logic excluded: 'How many cast we out that Christ receives in,' he asked.[21]

Although Rutherford rejected any suggestion of universalism he went to great lengths to emphasise the completeness of the atonement for the elect. The Cross not only brought reconciliation as the Arminians taught, but also meant that God was accessible to man, remission was available, the righteousness of God was vindicated and imputed to the believer.[22]

Justification for Rutherford, like election, was a sovereign act of God's free grace.[23] In his *Covenant of Life Opened*, he issued a warning against accepting Baxter's view, where repentance and works were set before justification.[24] Rutherford pointed out that man is not justified on account of his faith but by faith. 'Faith,' he declared, 'is no meritorious cause of right to remission and life eternal',[25] nor is it a measure of God's blessing in salvation, since 'a little hand with small fingers may receive a great heaven and lay hold on the great Saviour of the world'.[26] The merits of Christ confer no merits upon man as Arminians taught; it was 'because He loved us, He sent His Son in the flesh to die for us.'[27]

Rutherford's teaching on the perseverance of the saints sprang from the Calvinistic belief in election and the irresistible grace of God. '*Docimus perseventia esse effectum gratuitae electionis ad gloriam*,' he wrote.[28] Rutherford believed that saints cannot fall from glory. If they fell then God Himself had failed and the Cross was of no effect.[29] Associated with the doctrine of perseverance was that of assurance. This too issued from belief in election, since it is the elect who have assurance.[30] Believers may backslide but they never lose their assurance. Faith itself carries assurance, an assurance which is of the mind, the will, intelligence and affection. Blessings too which result from salvation, such as peace, glory in trial, loving hearts along with the witness of the Spirit all make for assurance.

The Protagonist of Presbyterianism

Rutherford not only championed the cause of Presbyterianism at Westminster, he recorded its abiding principles on paper. He has more right to be considered its voice than David Calderwood.* While Andrew Melville in the sixteenth century laid down its fundamental principles, Rutherford formulated it as a system of government in the seventeenth. Rutherford's ecclesiastical position was to a large extent decided by his rejection of Episcopacy on the one hand and his objection to Independency on the other. In his *Divine Right of Church Government and Excommunication*,

---

* David Calderwood (1575-1650), Scottish theologian and church historian.

Rutherford refuted the reliance of Thomas Hooker and William
Prynne* on reason, categorically stating that it was inconceivable
that God should leave anything to reason.[31] In *Due Right of
Presbyteries*, he supplied an answer to Hooker's *Way of the Church
and Christ in New England* and Robinson's *Justification of
Separation*, considering the institution and constitution of the
Church, the evil of separation, and the need for systematic
government within it. *Due Right of Presbyteries* was largely the
result of Rutherford's reaction to debates in the Westminster
Assembly; indeed he wrote it as the debates took place. Some
sections (such as pages 144–174) were inserted into the text after
hearing the debates which took place in November and December
1643. Pages 289–484 were also probably added as a result of what
Rutherford heard in the Assembly. This explains what Baillie
meant when he wrote of Rutherford's 'daily enlarging' of the
book.[32]

In his doctrine of the Church, Rutherford distinguished between
the visible and the invisible. The Church visible, he believed,
consisted of all who profess faith in Christ. Such a Church, he
argued, has ever existed since the time of the apostles. Even during
the Middle Ages there was a true Church visible within the
corruption of Rome. This belief he held in common with others,
but while for the majority faith was no more than assent to teaching,
for Rutherford it was personal commitment to Christ. He declared
that the Church invisible is the true Church, composed of the elect
with Christ as its Head. His doctrine of the visible Church brought
him into conflict with the Independents. Rutherford distinguished
between profession of faith and reality of conversion. He contended
that Independents made professing saints into real saints and that
no ecclesiastical authority could ask for more than profession. It
is the task of the Church, according to Rutherford, to make the
professing Christian into a real Christian. Rutherford thus pled
for a *via media* in saintliness. He avoided the excessive claims of

* Thomas Hooker (1586-1647), English Puritan who emigrated to New
England and wrote in defence of Congregationalism. William Prynne (1600-
1669), Presbyterian theologian and Member of Parliament who also held
Erastian views.

the Independents and at the same time any form of confirmation
as practised by the Episcopalians. Candidates for church
membership were required to give a straightforward profession
of faith, accompanied by loyalty and an earnest striving after
Christ. Membership was not the reward of an acquired saintliness,
but entry into a life of Christian endeavour. The Church was not a
gathered out company of saints, but a school of the aspiring.

   The relation of Church to State is largely dictated by the concept
of the Church that is held. It is a crucial issue in every age, and it
was particularly so in the seventeenth century. Rutherford was
strongly opposed to any form of Erastianism which in any way
compromised the spiritual independence of the Church. His
increasing intolerance of secular interference in ecclesiastical
affairs is revealed in his *Peaceable Plea, Due Right of Presbyteries*
and *Divine Right of Church Government*.

   Economic concerns, such as the regulation of imports and
exports and the fixing of the rate of exchange, Rutherford believed
to be the responsibility of the State and not that of the Church.
The petitioning of Parliament, however, for the relief of depressed
areas such as Argyll was the concern of the Kirk. It was permitted
to petition against oppressive economic legislation and even
engage in armed rebellion for religious and national causes,
although it was not the business of the Church to interfere in
military affairs. Rutherford concluded that Christ left 'no liberty
or latitude to magistrates or churches whatsoever to choose and
settle, such as an orderly form of church government or discipline
as is most suitable to their civil government.'[33] In his refutation of
the teaching of Erastus, Rutherford pointed out that the state has a
twofold duty; to direct men to do good and to punish the evildoer.[34]
The Church too, Rutherford believed, had a twofold task, but quite
different from that of the state: first and foremost to preach the
Word, and also to exercise discipline not only by persuasion but
also by means of definite acts of church control.

   The issue of Church and State came to prominence in the
excommunication debate. Erastus was eager to place the power
of excommunication in the hands of the civil magistrate, on the
ground that he was likely to be more impartial than any local

ecclesiastical court. Rutherford, on the contrary, saw excommunication as a matter solely for the Church. He argued that excommunication did not exclude men from heaven, nor did it separate them from the invisible body,[35] but it did involve 'a real internal supervision of the influence of His Spirit in Heaven'.[36] Rutherford rejected the notion that excommunication meant handing over to Satan to be hardened morally; rather, he contended it involved being 'softened that his spirit may be saved'.[37] In his reply to Erastus Rutherford did not distinguish between discipline and doctrine. While the pastor is subject to the magistrate, the magistrate as a Christian is subject to the pastor. If, however, the exercise of discipline was not a private affair, then there were grounds for Erastus' belief that it should be left to the magistrate. Rutherford believed there should be a harmonious relationship between magistrate and pastor, which he described as 'a reciprocation of subordinations, between the Church and the magistrate, a sort of collaterality and independent supremacy in their own kind to both'.[38] Rutherford was not prepared to concede any appeal from Church courts to the magistrate, but he believed a magistrate could pass judgement on procedure, though not on decision.

In his reply to Prynne, in the third section of the *Divine Right of Church Government and Excommunication*, Rutherford distinguished political Erastianism from its ecclesiastical counterpart. Rutherford maintained that the duty of the magistrates was to procure preachers and church officers to dispense the Word, the Sacrament and discipline, but the Church was to be the sole judge of their ability and faithfulness. The magistrate was, according to Rutherford, responsible for providing pastors' emoluments, but he had no power to arrest their wages. While he could punish preachers for preaching false doctrine, he was not in a position to decide as to what was false teaching. While a magistrate might exhort a man to faith he could not compel such.

At the heart of Presbyterianism, as the term suggests, is the presbytery. Rutherford defined and defended the place of the presbytery in his work the *Due Right of Presbyteries*. In it he did more than single out the presbytery as an agent of Church government – he considered the Presbyterian system as a whole.

While Rutherford contended earnestly for the right of the congregation to choose its own pastor, he asserted from the patristic Schoolmen that a congregation has no right to ordain its officers, since only administrative power resides in the local church.[39]

Rutherford taught that discipline should be imposed from outside and above men. He believed that by teaching and censure men are disciplined in the ways of God. Synods can possibly err, he conceded, but argued that they rarely did so. Fallible men are able to proclaim infallible truth. The Synod, composed of men under the guidance of the Spirit of God, was as perfect a body as anyone could desire. 'What Synods determine being the undeniable Word of God,' he wrote, 'is intrinsically infallible and can never become fallible, though fallible and sinful men that are obnoxious to error and mistakes do hold it forth ministerially to others.'[40] In this high doctrine of the Synod, Rutherford had in mind national conventions and covenants. National covenants imposed confessions, but Rutherford was prepared to allow that 'if people shall find their decrees truly to be so often trial they have power to reject them'.[41]

Another pillar of Presbyterianism is the elder. Eldership in its present form can be traced to Rutherford and Gillespie. The *Second Book of Discipline* denied the eldership any judicial power in the affairs of the congregation. Its function was laid down as pastoral and administrative, although the suggestion was made that a number of elders from several parishes could act judicially in local cases. It was generally held that the elder does not possess the power to ordain and consequently could not deprive a minister of his office, but the elder is a ruling officer in the Church, an affirmation which has saved the kirk session from becoming merely a committee of Presbytery, with no intrinsic power. This has allowed the kirk session to become the effective instrument it is in Presbyterianism.

When dealing with the office of minister Rutherford insisted upon the application of three principles: (1) ordination should be delayed until there has been election to a charge; (2) converting power lay in the pastor's office; (3) ordination permitted ministry in any Christian church. Rutherford was adamant that congregations had the right to elect freely their ministers, an affirmation which met with the wholehearted approval of the Independents at Westminster. Little did Rutherford realise that it was the application of this principle that was to be so sore a point of contention until the end of the nineteenth century and, before being resolved, to bring about the greatest disruption his beloved Church had ever witnessed. Rutherford not only insisted upon the freedom of the congregation to choose its pastor, but also he maintained that it was the right of every member to vote, not merely the heads of families, every woman as well as man. He argued that if a woman can exercise faith in Christ, then she has the right to participate in the election of a pastor. Once elected, however, Rutherford believed the pastor was freed from responsibility to the congregation in any pastoral act, although he had no special authority conferred at ordination. Rutherford opined that the power of the pastor is derived directly from Christ.

Rutherford first came into prominence as a champion of Presbyterianism by his resistance to the imposition of Episcopacy during his Anwoth ministry. To him it was 'the ceremonial faith'.[42] His protest at this time was mainly directed against prayer book, ceremonies and prelates whom he referred to as 'bastard porters' and 'irreverent bishops', responsible for the din and noise of ceremonies, holy days and other Romish corruptions'.[43] His encounter with Sydserff and his arraignment before the High Commission did not endear Episcopacy to him.[44] To Rutherford, Episcopacy was the near relation to popery: 'I am not a little grieved that our mother Church is running to the brothel house,' he wrote, 'and that we are hiring lovers, and giving gifts to the Great Mother of Fornications.'[45]

It was, however, through his debates with the Independents, particularly at Westminster, that Rutherford became the most prominent protagonist of Presbyterianism. He had no hesitation in rejecting the doctrine of an inner light. He saw in its subjectivism a danger to the community; the seed bed of anarchy. The downfall of Charles I and Laud created a vacuum in which the individualism of the seventeenth century could express itself. Rutherford made several references to the sectaries in his correspondence, bewailing

their existence, extremism and multiplicity in England.[46] Some of
the sects, such as the Baptists, often stigmatised as Anabaptists,
were relatively conservative. The Baptists were Independents as
far as church government was concerned, although they were never
so devoted to the principle of Independency as those who bore the
name, and were not averse to local association of churches even
to the point of connexionalism. They were called Baptists because
of their insistence upon 'believers' as opposed to 'infant baptism'.
Other sects were radical and extravagant. Antinomians, although
Calvinists, objected to the strict morality of Calvinism.[47] Seekers
can best be described as a charismatic group,[48] while Millenaries
and Chiliasts were as their names suggest, like the Fifth Monarchy
Men, eschatological in their emphasis. Frequent mention is made
of the Familists.[49] Their distinctive doctrines and practices are
difficult to discover. They may well have been a hybrid group
which included Quietists, Pantheists, Mystics and pseudo mystics.
Most extreme were the Anti-Sabbatarians, Soul Sleepers, Arians,
Socinians and Anti-Trinitarians. Thomas Edwards, in his rather
jumbled account of the sects entitled *Gangraena*, listed 170 errors,
while Robert Baillie in *Dissuasive from the errors of the Time*
included a catalogue of every sect from 1600 to 1660.

As the sects increased in number so did their demand for
toleration. Some demanded it for themselves alone, denying it to
others, while moderates were prepared to extend it to others who
differed from them. The strongest advocates of toleration were
the Baptists, the most famous protagonist of whom was Roger
Williams, the founder of Rhode Island Colony, which practised
universal suffrage and full liberty of conscience. Williams was
not prepared to set any limits upon toleration. Some Independents
such as Henry Barton and John Goodwin advocated toleration,
limiting it only by the right of the local congregation to deal with
error. Although in the main the Independents were not prepared
to be part of a national Church, they were prepared to tolerate it.
Others, like Nye, wanted a degree of toleration, which would
embrace themselves but exclude Episcopalians, Antinomians and
Arians, along with some heretical extremist groups. In 1644 the
Independents, in an effort to gain Army support, broadened their

concept of toleration, but drew the line at obvious heresy. While Rutherford commended the saintliness of the Independents he resolutely opposed their system of church government and belief in toleration. He categorically asserted in a letter to Lady Boyd that they were 'contrary to God's Word'[50] – they 'want God's word to warrant them'.[51] In a later letter he cited Thomas Goodwin and Jeremiah Burroughs, along with several others, whom he did not name, as 'mighty opposites to presbyterial government'.[52] It was with obvious satisfaction that he reported to Lady Boyd the progress Presbyterianism had made in the Westminster Assembly, the Presbyterial principle having been proved by reference to the churches in Jerusalem and Ephesus, along with the practice of ordination by presbytery rather than the single congregation, as was customary among the Independents. In happy anticipation he looked forward to a further Presbyterian triumph in the excommunication debate. Presbyterianism to Rutherford spelled order, Independency meant anarchy.[53]

The Political Philosopher
The tensions of the time drew Rutherford into the arena of political controversy. The relation between Crown and Church in Scotland had never been clearly defined. The effect of the confrontation between Mary Stuart and John Knox lingered on into the next century. Mary's son, James VI of Scotland, the first of the Stuarts to occupy the English throne, inherited his mother's doctrine of monarchy. Five years before the union of the crowns in 1603, James declared his concept of monarchy in a work entitled *Trew Law of Free Monarchies*. In it he insisted that monarchy should not be pressurised either from without a kingdom or by feudatories and sectaries from within. It was an attempt to expound the doctrine of the Divine Right of Kings. In view of James' treatment by the Scottish nobility before his elevation to the English throne, his thesis was justifiable. Rutherford was bound to come into conflict sooner or later with a monarch who exclaimed that 'A Scottish Presbytery agreeth as well with monarchy as God with the devil'. James went so far as to maintain that kings appointed by God were themselves Gods.[54]

James asserted that the King was the source of law and consequently above law. James' son and successor, Charles I, in the words of Godfrey Davies, 'did not share his father's fondness for abstract speculation nor his considerable literary and oratorical gifts; his views have to be gleaned, therefore, from occasional utterances not from full length discourses'.[55] For Charles, 'Rex' was 'Lex'.[56] Where James was content to theorise, Charles insisted upon putting principle into practice. Theory can be disputed, but practice can be provoking, especially when practice is by one who himself admitted that he could not defend a bad cause, nor yield in a good one.

Presbyterian insistence upon the spiritual independence of the Church meant that Crown and Church in Scotland were set upon collision courses. Monarchy in Scotland was different from that in England. In Scotland there had always been a democratic tradition. Celtic monarchy was elective. Bruce had ruled to a large extent by the will of the feudal overlords or clan chiefs. Major declared that in Scotland, 'the power of the king depends upon the whole people and they despise him for worthlessness and they elect another.'[57] He maintained that 'it was from the people; and most of all from the chief men and nobility who act for the common people that kings have their visitation'.[58]

Charles lived his life in England. He was out of touch with Scottish sentiment and tradition. A clash between Charles and the Kirk was inevitable, since he was not prepared to tolerate Presbyterianism, nor play a subservient role to the national Church. The conflict would have been less acrimonious if the monarch had been acquainted with the strength of Scottish feeling and the nature of its monarchical traditions.

It was Stuart pretensions that led Rutherford to pen *Lex Rex*, published anonymously in London in 1644. Row, in his *Life of Blair*, related that Rutherford submitted part of his manuscript to Blair,* and that Blair dissuaded him from publishing it. 'As for this subject, it being proper for juriconsults, lawyers and politicians,

---

* Robert Blair (1593-1666) who ministered in Ireland and subsequently in Ayr and St Andrews.

it lies out of your read. My advice to you is, that ye let it lie by you seven years, and busy your pen in writing that which will be more for edification and good of souls,' advised Blair.[59] At the time Rutherford followed Blair's counsel; not long after, however, he was persuaded by Warriston to complete the work with his assistance. Consequently it is impossible to say for sure how much of the work is solely that of Rutherford. It appears from the contents of the first part of *Lex Rex* – probably that studied by Blair[60] – that Rutherford's object was to justify the war waged against Charles. It could well have been written when papers of the Earl of Antrim exposed Charles' negotiations with the Irish in May 1643.[61] Argyll, who apparently was eager to depose the King, found a convenient ally in Rutherford.

   Lex Rex was the Presbyterian reply to Bishop Maxwell's publication of *Sacro-sancta Regum majestas.*[62] It was written at the time of the King's negotiations with Parliament at Oxford and Uxbridge, 1644-45. Presbyterians were demanding a reformation of religion according to the Covenant, a prescription of the King's supporters, and a nomination by Parliament to places of importance in Army and Navy. The demands were in the main drawn up by Warriston and presented to the King at Uxbridge in January, 1645. Charles was asked to take the Covenant and give the royal assent to the new *Directory of Public Worship. Lex Rex* is an expression of the philosophy that lies behind the proposals presented to the King. Patently they were unacceptable to a Stuart committed to Episcopacy and the Anglican liturgy. If Charles read *Lex Rex* then it must have been clear to him that he would need to abandon the doctrine of divine right to rule Scotland, and that was something Charles Stuart could never do. Theory and principle apart, the dominance of Argyll in Scotland made certain that Charles had no prospect of achieving his ends north of the border.

   Guthrie informs us that *Lex Rex* was circulated widely in the General Assembly of 1645.[63] It was republished in 1648, at the time of 'The Engagement',* with a new title, *The Pre-eminence*

---

* The Engagement was the secret agreement between some Scottish nobles and the imprisoned Charles by which the nobles undertook to raise an army to restore the king to the throne. (See Chapter 6.)

of the election of Kings. A further publication took place in 1657 concurrently with the 'Humble Petition and Advice', when it was entitled *A Treatise of Civil Polity.* On this occasion Cromwell was the arbitrary tyrant, not Charles.

The work commences with a discussion as to the origin of the state, along lines laid down by Aristotle. Rutherford believed that the impulse to establish the state is to be found in the social instinct of man, implanted in the heart by God. 'All civil power is immediately from God in its root,' he wrote.[64] He maintained too, after the manner of Bodin and Suarez,* that the family is the primitive form of state. Unlike Bodin, however, he drew democratic conclusions from this association rather than autocracy. While men, argued Rutherford in a typical Calvinistic manner, are born free, they are sinful and government is necessary to curb their evil propensities. Although man may rebel against his government, there is a moral instinct within him that desires it. This instinct is implanted by God, but forms of government are of men. Rutherford's political philosophy rests therefore upon two foundations, the *lex naturalis* and the *ius gentium.*

When Rutherford referred to natural law, he did not make it clear as to what precisely he meant by the term. He took it for granted that *lex naturalis* is a primary principle understood and obeyed by all. The result is that in Rutherford's writings the natural law is sometimes a practicable principle of life, while at others it is a politico-ethical concept.

Rutherford was more definite about the *ius gentium.* For him, it was a body of laws and practice, emerging from the distinctive life of peoples, which must ever be examined at the court of natural law. There was a further category of law for Rutherford, the *ius positivum,* the will of parliaments and peoples. It is not possible to change natural law, argued Rutherford; *ius gentium,* however, he contended can be changed, but only after serious thought and deliberation. The object of the state, he declared, must ever be 'the people's good in a quiet and peaceable life of godliness and honesty'.[65]

---

* Jean Bodin, (1530-96), French political theorist. Francisco de Suarez (1548-1617), Spanish Jesuit philosopher.

Rutherford's doctrine of kingship rested upon the *ius gentium*. He saw it as a gift from God, the people's part being the application of the man to the office. Election, he insisted, should be entrusted to the Three Estates, as representatives of the people, rather than the populace itself. While he accepted a theory of Divine Right based upon Deuteronomy 17, he limited royal power by law and election. Divine right owed nothing to natural law. Rutherford was careful to distinguish between paternal and regal power, the latter being derived from the *ius gentium*.[66] For Rutherford, as for many of his contemporaries, monarchy was a contract between King and people. He set great store upon the words of 2 Kings 11:17, where it is stated that Jehoiada made a covenant between the Lord and the King and people, that they should be the Lord's people involved in a contract with the King. Royalists like Maxwell accepted a contractual theory of monarchy, but they maintained that an integral part of the contract was the surrender of the people's power to the sovereign. In agreement with Locke, Rutherford viewed Charles' coronation oath as a covenant, but went further by opposing the veto of an upper house, which was quite understandable in view of his intense dislike of the Scottish upper house, described as a composition of 'rotten men'.[67] According to Rutherford, the King's power was 'but a birthright of the people borrowed from them, that they might let it out for their good and resume it when a man is drunk with it'.[68] Likewise, he argued, judges derive their authority from the people and must be free from royal influence, supporting his argument by reference to Scottish laws prohibiting the King from interfering with legal judgements.[69] Judges, he asserted, were to be the sole interpreters of law.[70]

In the light of his theory, the war for Rutherford was a defensive operation.[71] Armed resistance to Charles was justified on the ground that he was a tyrant who had broken his coronation oath to defend the Protestant religion and govern peaceably in its interest. Rutherford claimed that Charles had acted unconstitutionally in raising an army and declaring war without the consent of Parliament. In this Rutherford was at one with the English Common Lawyers, but he was not prepared to make Ship Money a *casus belli*. 'It is better to yield in a matter of goods,' he wrote, 'than to come to arms.'[72]

Self-defence for him was part of the *Lex naturalis*, it being 'a mighty defect in Providence if dogs by nature may defend themselves against wolves, bulls against lions – and man in the absence of lawful magistrates may not defend himself against unjust violence'.[73] When life and religion are in jeopardy then any people have a right to armed resistance, but it is the duty of a Christian first to resort to supplication, next attempt flight, and only finally resist to death. Scotland had tried supplication; patently flight was impossible; so that armed resistance was the course left open. He was prepared to concede resistance to King or Parliament where the *ius gentium* was concerned, such as acts against life and liberty and detrimental to the principles of Common law.

Rutherford rejects the notion that the Christian should take the path of non-resistance.[74] Certainly Christ had taken this course, but Rutherford argued this was His prerogative. It is our prerogative to offer resistance to evil. Rutherford found that his advocacy of resistance did not have the support of the Fathers; accordingly he sought refuge in the opinions of such Reformers as Beza and Buchanan, although there is little attempt on his part to support his contention with citations from those he supposed advocated active resistance. Rutherford firmly believed that non-resistance was a sure way of fostering tyranny.

When it was argued that that was evil, Rutherford was quick to reply that it could sometimes be justified as righteous resistance to evil. Here he was without the scriptural backing he would have wished. We find him quite out of character declaring that 'practice in scripture is a narrow rule of faith'.[75] Rutherford was forced in the main to turn to the Old Testament for support in his advocacy of resistance, although he did not entirely ignore the New. He found in Romans 13 what he believed to be sufficient authority for a doctrine of resistance, but he rested particularly on the apostle's statement that rulers are a terror to evildoers. He denounced Charles Stuart as a terror to good. No claim can be made for originality in Rutherford's political philosophy. His doctrines of limited monarchy, elective crown and a free judiciary were highlighted by the backcloth of Stuart pretensions. Rutherford had the keen sense to detect inconsistencies and employ them to advantage.

The Correspondent

Rutherford won fame as a letter writer in his lifetime. Sixty of his letters were written from Anwoth during the period of his pastoral ministry in Galloway, but the vast majority, two hundred and twenty in all, belong to the eighteen months of confinement in Aberdeen. The reason for this epistolary activity in the 'Granite City' is not difficult to understand. The letter was the only means he had of keeping in touch with his many acquaintances and friends. Rutherford was also much concerned as to the welfare of his flock in Anwoth. By pen he counselled them, and sought to strengthen their resistance to the imposition of the Prayer Book and Episcopacy.[76] His aim was ever to support the Presbyterian cause. Many of his letters addressed to the wives of lairds and dignitaries were written that they might employ their female charms on their husbands in support of Presbyterianism. Sixty of the Aberdeen letters were addressed to ladies of social standing.

As Rutherford's literary fame grew, letter followed letter in swift succession. No matter what the primary motive for writing – pastoral, personal or propagandist – every letter was shot through with the evangelical faith. While the pastoral letters were Pauline in form, the propagandist productions were written in the style of 'testimonies', developed by the French Huguenots.

The letters were sent to a wide variety of folk in very different professions and social standing. Among his addressees were soldiers, ministers, lairds, wives of nobles as well as those of humbler sort.

The great majority of Rutherford's letters were penned to the aristocracy, Lords Boyd, Craighall, Balmerino, Lindsay of Byres, Loudon; Earls Lothian and Cassillis. Among the nobility, his principal correspondents were the Gordons of Earlston and Knockbreck. Four were written to Alexander Gordon of Earlston, the same number was addressed to Robert Gordon of Knockbreck. He also wrote four to the elder John Gordon of Cardoness, and three to the younger of that name. While in these letters to the nobility there are occasional references to national events, such as the introduction of Episcopalian ceremonies,[77] church desolation[78] and prelacy,[79] he was mainly concerned with Christian character and public conduct. Occasionally, Rutherford referred to the privilege of witnessing for Christ.[80] He realised that there was always a strong and insidious temptation for the nobility to curry favour with the King at the expense of their faith; hence his warnings as to the emptiness of the world,[81] dishonouring compliances,[82] dangers from the fear and favours of men[83] and ambition.[84] Rutherford stressed to his addressees that the only sure safeguard against backsliding was death to the world for Christ's sake,[85] exertions in His cause[86] and the winning of the Saviour at all costs.[87] No one knew more than Rutherford how much the nobility stood in need of encouragement in those days of religious strife and political contention.[88]

Chief among Rutherford's female correspondents was Marion McNaught, daughter of the Laird of Kilquharrie, and wife of William Fullarton, Provost of Kirkcudbright, a woman renowned for her saintliness and support of the Presbyterian cause. Bonar, in his preface to the sixth letter, records that it was not until 1860 that her house in Kirkcudbright was removed, and that in the town's churchyard there once stood a tombstone bearing the inscription,[89]

Marion McNaught, sister to John McNaught of Kilquhanatie, an ancient and honourable baron, and spouse to William Fullerton, Provost of Kirkcudbright, died April 1643, aged 58.

Sexum animis, piete genus, gerosa, locumque
Virtute exsuperans, conditur hoc tumulo.

No less than forty-four letters were addressed to her. Prior to Rutherford's removal to Aberdeen in 1636, she was his principal correspondent, thirty-five out of fifty-seven letters being addressed to her. She was Rutherford's confidante. To her, a mother of three children, he wrote much of children, their dedication to God,[90] their place in the family,[91] and Christ's care for those of believers.[92] It was to Marion McNaught he unburdened his heart at the time of his wife's illness.[93] No heart could have been more sensitive to the agony of Scotland than that of Marion McNaught. Rutherford shared with her his deep concern. To her he wrote of the introduction of the hated service book, the troubles of the Kirk, and his own banishment to Aberdeen.[94] It was to Marion McNaught that he commended a mother of several children, who was facing death, with the assurance that no one was more able to console the poor woman than the wife of the Provost of Kirkcudbright.[95]

Another confidante of Rutherford was Lady Kenmure, to whom he wrote some fifty-six letters in all, mostly in the earlier part of his life. Lady Kenmure was the third daughter of Archibald Campbell, seventh Earl of Argyll. Like Marion McNaught she earned a reputation for piety and devotion to Presbyterianism.[96] Rutherford sustained her in her life of sorrow occasioned by the death of her husband in 1634, at the early age of thirty-five; the deaths in 1629 and 1634 of her daughters in infancy,[97] and the death of her son in August, 1649. Her second marriage proved to be hardly less fraught with sorrow, her second husband, the Hon. Sir Henry Montgomery of Giffin, predeceasing her. A comparison of these letters to Lady Kenmure with those addressed to Marion McNaught show little difference in style and content. He shared with Lady Kenmure the sorrow of his wife's death[98] and that of his removal from Anwoth.[99] Rutherford reveals his ability as a counsellor in his correspondence with Lady Kenmure, and we note too that her sorrow drew from Rutherford's pen a number of comments on the ministry of affliction in a believer's life.[100]

Seven letters were addressed to Lady Boyd, who before her first marriage to Lord Lindsay of Byres was Christian Hamilton, the eldest daughter of Thomas, first Earl of Haddington. Like Marion McNaught and Viscountess Kenmure, she too was renowned for her saintliness and devotion to the Presbyterian cause.[101] To Lady Boyd Rutherford wrote of his sad lack of fellowship in Aberdeen.[102] It was to Lady Boyd he wrote of the grace that had sustained him in the hostile city,[103] and the lessons he learned in adversity.[104]

Four letters were despatched to Lady Culross, Elizabeth Melville, daughter of Sir James Melville of Hallhill in Fife. She gained a reputation as a poetess of religious verses.[105] Also among Rutherford's titled female correspondents were Ladies Cardoness,[106] Largirie,[107] Busbie,[108] Rowallan,[109] Mar,[110] Hallhill,[111] Gaitgirth,[112] Craighall,[113] Dungueigh,[114] and Kilconquhair.[115]

We find Rutherford also writing to humbler womenfolk such as Margaret Ballantyne, whom Bonar thinks may have been a parishioner of Anwoth;[116] two unidentified gentlewomen, a Jean Brown and a Jean Macmillan,[117] along with a Bethsaida Aird who, like Margaret Ballantyne, may well have been a member of the church in Anwoth.

Rutherford carried on a correspondence with a number of fellow ministers. Like him they too faced persecution for conscience sake. It is not surprising that he sought to encourage them in their resistance to Stuart impositions. He counselled Hugh McKail to trust Christ amid trial.[118] To David Dickson, who in 1618 became minister of Irvine, he testified that the bitterness of life is often sweetened.[119] He wrote of his own suffering as a 'sugared cross'.[120] He reminded a Glasgow minister that 'there was a necessity' laid on him to preach the gospel and call people to a covenant of grace.[121] Writing to James Guthrie of Stirling, he called for steadfastness in persecution.[122]

There is, however, comparatively little reference in his correspondence with fellow ministers to contemporary religious events. In a letter to John Livingstone, the first minister of Kilsyth, Rutherford referred to his removal from Anwoth and confinement in Aberdeen along with the projected reconciliation with the Lutherans,[123] but he was far more eager to extol the glories of Christ.[124] It is not surprising, therefore, that in writing to William Dalgleish, the neighbouring minister of Kirkdale and Kilmabreck, he wrote, 'Let the conquest of souls be top and root, flower and blossom of your joys and desires on this side of sun and moon',[125] while in a letter to James Hamilton, a fellow Scot in County Down, he confessed that his supreme delight was preaching the gospel: 'My one joy,' he wrote, 'next to the flower of my joys, Christ, was to preach my sweetest Master, and the glory of His Kingdom.'[126]

Every student of Rutherford is indebted to Bonar for his editions of the *Letters*, but unfortunately Bonar was not as accurate in his dating as he might have been. Letter XLVIII, addressed to Marion McNaught from Edinburgh, dated December 1634, refers to the death of the King of Sweden,[127] which occurred in 1632. Letter XXXVI,[128] again addressed to Marion McNaught from Anwoth requesting her assistance in the choice of a commissioner, and dated May 20th 1634, rightly belongs to the previous year, possibly early in that year rather than as late as May. Letter XLI,[129] to Marion McNaught, written from Edinburgh and dated 1634, referring to the attempt to bring about redress of grievances in connection with the imposition of Episcopacy, belongs also either to 1633 or even 1632, the period when the Presbyterian cause was being pressed by several of its champions in the capital.[130] Judging from a reference to Rutherford's call by Cramond, it is possible that the undated letter XLIII[131] to Marion McNaught also belongs to this time, Cramond being vacant in 1633. Further, the suggested compromise points to the episcopate of the kindly Lamb, rather than the hostile Sydserff, who became bishop in 1634. The undated letter XLVII,[132] yet another addressed to Marion McNaught placed with the correspondence of 1634, also seems to be misplaced. It makes reference to Dickson's settlement in Irvine, which took place in the first half of 1633, a conclusion which is confirmed by the fact that Gordon is referred to as Lochinvar. If Rutherford had written this letter in 1634, as Bonar believed, then no doubt he would have referred to Gordon as Kenmure.

Rutherford appeared upon the stage of history at a time when the Scottish language was fast being anglicised. By the mid-sixteenth century there was a distinct contrast between the language of the Highlands and that of the Lowlands. The conclusion of the 'auld alliance' with France and the cessation of armed hostility with England contributed much to the supremacy of the English tongue north of Solway and Tweed. Much more, the union of the crowns in 1603 popularised the English tongue in Scotland. Though for so long potentially linked with France, the Scottish language never admitted the same volume of French words as did the Anglo-Saxon tongue during the Norman French domination. English, during the seventeenth century in Scotland, soon became the language of elite society. 'From the union of the crowns it became the ambition of educated Scotsmen to write, and to be able to speak the literary English of the court of the south.'[133] Increasingly the braid Scots was heard only on the tongue of the peasant. Scotticisms were for centuries to be heard and read and indeed still are, but by the middle of the seventeenth century the Scots were more adept at writing than speaking the English language.

The great age of Scottish literature had not yet come in Rutherford's time. It had to wait until the following century. The seventeenth century, however, was one of England's greatest periods of literature. It was the age of Raleigh, Bacon, Milton and above all Shakespeare. Scotland at this time had little of which to boast. Robert Aytoun (1570-1649), the courtier, was a poet of some renown; as indeed were the Earls of Stirling (1567-1640) and Ancrum (1578-1654), but only William Drummond (1585-1649) achieved any widespread fame. Rutherford along with Leighton* ranks highly as a devotional writer of the century.

Douglas Bush described the early seventeenth century as a period of 'mercantilism and mysticism'.[134] It was indeed such in England, but in Scotland the age of mercantilism was just beginning. If it was not an age of mercantilism it was certainly that of mysticism. The language of Rutherford is not dissimilar to that of other writers of the period. His biblical style and language are paralleled in Cromwell's letter to the Church of Scotland in which he besought them 'in the bowels of Christ' that they might be mistaken.[135] The similarity is even more marked in the poems of the English ecclesiastic John Donne, although he moved on a different level from Rutherford. In Donne, as in Rutherford, there is the same pre-occupation with Christ as Bridegroom and the Church as Bride. 'Show me, dear Christ, Thy spouse, so bright, so clear,' wrote the English poet.[136] Rutherford's zealous Protestantism is echoed in Thomas Fuller's comment that 'a little skill in antiquity inclines a man to Popery; but depth in that study brings him about again to our religion',[137] as also in the words from Hobbes' *Leviathan*, 'The Papacy is no other than the ghost of the deceased Roman Empire sitting crowned upon the grave thereof.'[138]

---

* Robert Leighton (1611-84), Archbishop of Glasgow, 1670-74.

A careful examination of the contents of Rutherford's letters reveals that the vast majority are concerned with the person and work of Christ in some way or other. The course of all the believer's enjoyment of Christ rests in the abundant provision God has made for men in Christ, Rutherford declared. In correspondence with Matthew Mowat, the Kilmarnock minister, Rutherford wrote of the 'running over love of Christ'.[139] In other letters, too, Rutherford made mention of the love of Christ.[140]

It is surprising that in view of Rutherford's exultant references to the love of Christ, there is little written of the Cross, but much of crosses, particularly his own. For Rutherford even the Cross of Christ had become his own.[141] No doubt it was because of his suffering and that of others for the cause of Christ, that suffering was a frequent subject for his pen. Tribulation was the unenviable lot of God's people.[142] Christ's suffering was not only redemptive but exemplary. Christ, for Rutherford, was ever a pattern in suffering.[143] Rutherford examined the causes of suffering. Sometimes, he believed, it arises from inward conflict, caused by outward trial.[144] At other times it springs from without, the perfidy of false brethren,[145] public wrongs and temptations.[146] That Christ never deserted His suffering people, Rutherford was assured. Christ was ever with them in the furnace of affliction. 'Know you not that Christ wooeth His wife in the Burning Bush?' he wrote to Marion McNaught.[147] Consequently he encouraged his readers to suffer for Christ, as he did Provost Fullarton of Kirkcudbright in his resistance to Sydserff's attempt to incarcerate William Glendinning, the town's minister.[148] Every affliction, Rutherford believed, brought with it needed grace; indeed he went so far as to maintain that 'grace groweth best in winter'.[149] Rutherford made it clear that there is no affliction without a divine purpose.[150] Trial could be a blessing in disguise for the believer.[151]

CHAPTER 6

THE PROTESTER

Rutherford's literary activity, especially in defence of the Presbyterian cause, brought him renown. Several unsolicited honours were conferred upon him. In 1649, the University of Edinburgh invited him to become its professor of theology, but such was his modesty that he pled with its Lord Provost to select 'some fitter man'.[1] The Assembly came to Rutherford's rescue by declining to countenance the move. St. Andrews was fortunate in retaining his services, first as Principal of the new College, and then as Rector of its university. In the previous year, the Dutch university of Harderwyck wanted him to occupy their chair of Divinity and Hebrew, and twice in 1651 Utrecht invited him to settle there. Rutherford was not ungrateful for the interest shown in him, and did not refuse these invitations without much prayer and heart searching, particularly the call to Utrecht. Such was his love for Scotland and its Kirk, he could not bring himself to part from them, especially at a time when there was an opportunity 'to build the waste places of Zion'.

Roots of Discord in the Presbyterian Ranks

The days that followed Rutherford's return to St. Andrews saw him busy with many mundane but vital matters of the Kirk. In 1648 he was appointed by the Assembly to a committee whose business it was 'to consider present dangers'.[2] Three days later, along with others, he was delegated to spread the appointment of diets, so that the Commission* might deal with tithes, the establishment of churches and the settlement of ministers.[3] Within

---

* A Commission of the General Assembly consisted of several members of the Assembly and exercised the powers of the Assembly in regard to any business committed to it by the Assembly. Between annual meetings of the Assembly, a Commission exercised oversight of church business.

the same week he was called upon to confer with the Chancellor, and in the following week he was requested to lead Parliament in its devotions.[4] On May 1st of the same year he heard the report of the Commission from Ireland.[5] Rutherford was as able in committee as in the pulpit and in the Assembly of Divines. It was not surprising therefore that in the summer of 1648 he was charged with the task of dealing with the 'Public Affaires of the Kirk'.[6] In the following year Rutherford was appointed to yet further committees, one to consider the problem of Orkney;[7] another, the 'prosecution of the covenant'.[8] In 1647 he had been given the unenviable task of remonstrating with the leaders of the nation for their defeat in war, for not seeking the guidance of the Kirk in their military campaign.

Rutherford was ever an opponent of patronage. In 1649, along with John Livingstone, James Guthrie, Patrick Gillespie* and Alexander Pierson, he drew up a petition to Parliament requesting its abolition.[9] The petition was completed by January 30th and approved by the Commission, which, on February 14th, appointed Rutherford and James Wood to justify their opposition to patronage.[10] On February 28th, Parliament was again petitioned by the Commission to discharge patronage, with the result that Rutherford had the satisfaction of witnessing its abolition by Parliament nine days later. Having achieved his object, Rutherford absented himself from the meeting of the Commission until the Assembly of 1649.

Distress, however, quickly followed upon the heels of duty for Rutherford. The turn of political events found him embroiled in bitter controversy with many of his erstwhile friends. After his defeat in the civil war, the wily Charles Stuart sought to play off his enemies one against another. He surrendered to the Scots, hoping that they would take pity on him, in spite of his harsh treatment of them. He knew that he could expect little mercy from the English Parliament, and none from the Army. Charles' hope that the Scots would rally to him was not without foundation.

---

* Patrick Gillespie (1617-75), minister at Kirkcaldy and Glasgow, and author of two treatises on covenant theology. He was the younger brother of George Gillespie (1613-48) who was a commissioner at the Westminster Assembly.

There were many in Scotland who vainly hoped for a settlement based upon the king's acceptance of the Covenant. Consequently, while Charles was in Carisbrooke Castle, on the Isle of Wight, they entered into what is known as the Engagement with him. Probably it was drawn up by Lanark and Lauderdale,* the latter having turned Royalist, the former assuring the Kirk of Charles' fidelity. Having been signed and sealed by December 27th, 1647, it was encased in lead and buried until such time as it could be safely transferred.

The Engagement was a specious arrangement between sovereign and subjects containing concessions which neither had any authority to make, and pledges which they had not power to perform. Charles insisted that although he made pledges he was in no way obliged to perform them. Few were convinced by the flowing words which were supposed to assure the Scots of Charles' willingness to preserve Presbyterianism, or indeed of the King's promise to establish it in England, provided that they restored him to power and permitted the use of the service book for his royal household. Wise heads in Scotland with a knowledge of Charles' character saw that he was employing them as a pawn in his own game, with no intention of recognising the Covenant if restored. Even the architects of the Engagement were dissatisfied with it. Lauderdale saw it merely as a temporary expedient, for Loudon it was too extreme, while Lanark did not think it went far enough. George Gillespie was loud in his denunciation of it, and found himself leader of the anti-Engagement party, ably supported by James Guthrie, and assisted by David Dickson, Robert Blair and Patrick Gillespie. When Rutherford returned from London in November 1647, he threw in his lot with those opposed to the Engagement.

The Engagement, however, was not rejected without careful consideration. When Lanark, Loudon and Lauderdale returned from England in February 1648, they gave a preliminary report to the Committee of Estates on the 10th of that month. It was Loudon's task to give an account of the negotiations which took

---

* The Western Remonstrance was drawn up by the leaders of the Covenanter army under Colonels Strachan and Ker.

place before the King's escape, Lauderdale explained the Engagement, while Lanark concluded the proceedings on the 15th. Three days later the Commission appointed a sub-committee of the Estates. Commission and Estates subsequently found themselves at issue over the Engagement. When the Commission was about to issue a declaration condemning it, the Estates asked that no such declaration be made without reference to the Committee of Estates. The Commission was in no mood to comply with the request of the Estates.[11] A meeting of Lanark, Lauderdale and Loudon with church leaders on February 28th and 29th served to harden the Kirk's opposition.[12] The Commission's declaration made clear that the Church's main objection to the Engagement was Charles' lack of commitment to the Covenant, and his partiality for Episcopacy. Could a Stuart, who had vowed on November 16th, 1647, and reaffirmed in a letter to the Commons dated December 28th, that he would not abolish Episcopacy, be trusted? The Commission also took exception to the omission of Prelacy, Popery and Erastianism from the list of heresies cited.[13] The Kirk felt it was justified in maintaining that the Covenant was threatened by both Independents and Malignants.

Parliament, on receiving the declaration, embarked upon a policy of delay, asking for time to consider it, and suggesting a fast.[14] The Commission was not prepared to countenance any delay and the fast was rejected. To the Kirk the issue was vital. On the following Sunday the declaration was read in every parish.[15] Within three days the Commission appointed a sub-committee to confer with a deputation from the Estates. The threat of war caused Parliament to turn its attention to matters of defence, to the annoyance of the Commission. When, by 22nd March, no satisfaction had been received from Parliament, the Commission presented it with what was known as the 'Eight Desires', as a basis for discussion. In these the Commission demanded that no declaration of war be made without reference to the Church and that clear reasons be set out for such action. The 'Desires' also adamantly refused the help of malignants, and called upon the Estates to state categorically that Charles' offer was unacceptable, unless he was prepared to accept the Covenant, to fully establish

Presbyterianism, to enforce the use of the Directory of Worship and Confession of Faith in all his dominions, and to take an oath that he would never retract his word.

The political situation became more complicated by reason of the demands which the Scottish Parliament made upon England. The Scottish Estates insisted upon a compulsory imposition of the Covenant, a complete purge of heresies, the disbanding of the Army, the restoration of expelled Presbyterian members of Parliament, and freedom for Charles to negotiate. The Commission took strong exception to the Estates' unreasonable demands, a protest which led to the publication of *The Humble Representation of the Commission of the General Assembly to the Honourable Estates of Parliament upon their Declaration lately communicated to us*.[16] While Patrick Gillespie and James Guthrie may have been its architects, the policy expressed in the document was that of Rutherford. In it, the Kirk made clear that it was not opposed to an Engagement with Charles to liberate England from the bondage of Independency, but that it doubted Charles' sincerity to do so, and pointed out that Parliament had no power to effect the establishment of Presbyterianism in England. Further, the *Representation* was sent by the Commission to all presbyteries.[17] The Commission's action resulted in a confrontation between Kirk and Parliament, the Estates maintaining on 11th May that political matters were their preserve. The Kirk's reply was expressed in what was called the 'Humble Vindication', in which it denied that its action was treasonous, employing Rutherford's argument from *Lex Rex*, that if Parliament erred, the people had a right to rectify the matter.

The defeat of the Scots, under the command of the Duke of Hamilton at Preston on 17th August, 1649, put an end to any such arrangement envisaged by the Engagement and made Charles' execution inevitable. In England power lay with the Army, while in Scotland, the stand of those who opposed the Engagement was vindicated. The anti-Engagement party was in no mood to treat its opponents kindly, and readily took the opportunity of persuading Parliament to pass the Act of Classes, debarring from civil and military position all supporters of the Engagement. Rutherford made it clear to the nation where he stood on the issue. Maintaining that 'Evil in the lump' incurred the wrath of God, he expressed his concern that 'sundrie brethren are found in clandestine meetings, having drawn up and subscribed papers which they purposed to have given into the Assembly, teaching to complyance with the sinful Engagement'; and in a letter from Fife he accused the Perth Presbytery of holding such meetings.[18] Rutherford, by reason of his outspokenness, was an obvious choice for the Assembly Committee appointed on January 5th, 1649, to negotiate with Parliament over the Engagement.

Charles' execution on 30th January, 1649, brought about a revulsion of feeling in his favour. The loyalty of the Scots to the House of Stuart was stirred to its depths, regardless of the way in which the late king had so arrogantly dismissed their appeals for the preservation of Presbyterianism. The blame for Charles' death was laid at the feet of the Army, whose ranks were largely recruited from the Independents. Covenanters found themselves in an embarrassing predicament. The Covenant demanded a King, and called for loyalty to Scotland's legitimate sovereign. Six days after his father's execution, the young Charles Stuart, while in Holland, was proclaimed king, but the passage of an Act through Parliament made his kingship provisional upon the acceptance of the Covenants. The son was no more disposed towards the Covenants than the father had been. Argyll wrote to the Prince of Orange pleading with him to persuade Charles to accept the Covenant.[19] Royalists in Paris considered it highly doubtful that Charles would agree to his Scottish subjects' demands and despaired 'of any successe of his treaty with the Scots'.[20] Charles pinned his faith on an invasion of Scotland by Montrose from Norway,[21] and Ormonde from Ireland. Cromwell, however, defeated Ormonde in September and October of 1649, and Charles reluctantly was forced to listen to Argyll, spokesman of the Covenanters. Charles cautiously played for time. Winram approached him in December, but on January 11th, 1650, was sent back with a request for a commissioner. There was still Montrose, and for his encouragement, the following day, January 12th, Charles sent him the Garter.[22] Charles must have wondered whether the Scottish crown was worth the price of the Covenanting terms: acceptance of the Covenants; establishment of Presbyterianism in England; recognition of the Act of Classes; enforcement of penal laws against Roman Catholics; and annulment of all treaties contrary to those laws and commissions prejudicial to the Covenant.

In view of the unveiled hatred he had for the Scots,[23] it is surprising that he considered the Covenanters' terms for more than a month. His main concern was for Montrose. He insisted upon an indemnity for him, providing that he laid down his arms.[24] When the Covenanters agreed to this, Charles accepted their terms, Sir William Fleming being given the unenviable task of receiving Montrose's submission. Charles, however, with customary Stuart guile, encouraged Montrose to resist. The defeat of Montrose at Carbisdale on 27th April and his subsequent execution left Charles with no alternative but to comply with the Covenanters' demands. In this he was encouraged by wiser heads; 'Scotland is worth but little if it be not worth the Covenant,' the Prince of Orange wrote to him.[25] Even his mother, Henrietta Maria, who later disapproved of his terms with the Scots,[26] counselled him 'to agree with them upon any tearmes, that he may by that meanes get possession, and a place upon which to set his foot, and then free himself at the first opportunity'.[27] Charles was justified in complaining that 'a declaration was extorted'[28] from him, especially when, after the defeat of Montrose, while *en route* for Scotland, he was presented with what was described as 'new and higher propositions'. He was tempted to alter course and land in Denmark, but 'overcome with the intreatyes of his servants who laid before him the present sad conditions of his affaires he yielded',[29] signing the declaration in which the terms were laid down on June 23rd. Consequently, when he landed at Speymouth, he did so as a covenanted king to be crowned at Scone on January 1st, 1651, at the hands of Argyll.

Argyll's vision of Charles as a Covenanting king was an unrealisable ideal. The Scots found 'nothing but vanity and lightness in him', they despaired of him ever proving to be 'a strenuous defender of their faith'.[30] Charles was more successful turning moderate Covenanters into Royalists than Argyll was of converting Charles to the Covenants. The Kirk did not take kindly

to Charles' love of dancing, his liking for the service book, and
his insistence upon kneeling at communion, although the Assembly
made no vocal protest. The defeat of Alexander Leslie's weakened
Covenanter army, purged of good officers and fighting men, at
Dunbar on 2nd and 3rd September, proved critical for Charles
and the Covenanters. Argyll found himself no longer able to ignore
those who had supported the Engagement. The army at Stirling
was useless, while in the west, when Colonel Gilbert Ker was
defeated by General Lambert at Hamilton on 1st December,
Colonel Strachan deserted to Cromwell. If Scotland was to rally
around Charles and resist the military pressure of Cromwell, then
the help of the Engagers was vital. In March, the Estates voted in
favour of the appointment of Engagers to the Army Committee, a
decision to which the General Assembly gave reluctant approval,
and on 2nd June the Act of Classes was repealed. The ascendancy
of Argyll was over. While Cromwell marched northwards from
the east, the Scots in the west, led by Charles, moved south into
England, only to be defeated on 3rd September at Worcester. The
flight of Charles after the battle brought to an end the dream of a
Covenanted king upon a Scottish throne.

Political and military events brought religious repercussions,
dividing the Presbyterian ranks. The rift between Engagers and
Anti-Engagers can be traced back to a meeting in Edinburgh's
West Kirk. Charles was asked to confess that the civil war was
the result of the sins of his house. Patrick Gillespie wanted to
make this a condition of military assistance. At the mercy of the
Scots, on August 16th, 1650, Charles accepted a Commission's
disclaimer which had been sanctioned by the Committee of Estates.
The defeat of the purged army at Dunbar made the acceptance of
royalists and their fellow travellers a necessity, bedfellows whom,
in happier circumstances, the Covenanters would not have
entertained. To Charles, the defeat at Dunbar was a fortunate
circumstance; Rutherford viewed it as a Divine judgement upon a
compromising nation. Those who shared Rutherford's sentiments
called for a further purging of the army, while their opponents
claimed that the army had been seriously weakened by
overpurging.

Course of the Conflict between Protesters and Resolutioners
The Western Remonstrance* drafted at Dumfries was submitted to the Commission on October 16th, 1650.[31] 'After some debate,' Baillie wrote, 'the draft of the Remonstrance is brought to some perfection'.[32] We cannot be sure who penned it. Warriston in his diary denied that he had done so, but even if he did not actually write it, he was a party to it. The Remonstrance was a recitation of the weakness of the Estates and Charles' insincerity with regard to the Covenant. The drafting of the Remonstrance was occasioned by another politico-religious party, the 'Remonstrants', as its members were called. Although closely allied to the Protesters, they were not identical with them, many of the Remonstrants later serving under Cromwell. While the Remonstrance was being drafted, Rutherford was in Fife, busily occupied with the work of the Commission. At Perth and Stirling he investigated the oppression of the ill-paid soldiers, and the profanity of the King's Lifeguards.

The Commission, at Perth and Stirling, appointed a committee, which included Rutherford, to consider the Remonstrance. Rutherford was sympathetic to it, believing that in the main it was a truthful statement of fact. The Commission, however, saw it in a different light, maintaining that it was a threat to Church unity.[33] Rutherford pointed out to Ker that he feared the Remonstrants would come to terms with Cromwell, accordingly he was eager to reconcile the Remonstrants with the ecclesiastical and political government. In this he failed, and found himself forced into the extremists' camp.

Covenanting sentiments had ever been strong in the west. There was no difficulty in raising an army in that quarter of the country. The defeat of the western army by Lambert at Hamilton on December 1st, 1650, was a bitter blow to both Remonstrants and the Commission. Patently an army was needed if the armed might of Independency was to be held at bay. The question was, should the recruiting net be cast wide enough to include Engagers? On December 14th Parliament presented an inquiry to the Commission

---

* The Western Remonstrance was drawn up by the leaders of the Covenanter army under Colonels Strachan and Ker.

asking, 'What persons are to be admitted to rise in arms?'[34] The
Commission, keen to heal the breach in Presbyterian ranks, and
put a strong army in the field, was in favour of including 'all
sensible persons...', excluding the 'excommunicate,... notoriously
profane...flagitious and such as have been from the beginning and
continue still obdurate and professed enemies and opposers of the
covenant and cause of God'.[35] The Commission's 'Resolution'
coincided with that of Parliament to relax political censures. A
copy of the resolution was sent to the presbyteries, together with
an act censuring those who supported Cromwell. The 'Resolution'
did not meet with widespread national approval. The presbyteries
of Ayr, Glasgow, Aberdeen, Paisley and Stirling maintained that
the 'Resolution' separated the issue of defence from that of the
Covenant.

In January, 1651, the Commission met in St. Andrews.
Rutherford attended the opening day's session although he served
on none of its committees, and subscribed to none of its documents.
He had no heart for this business, nor was he at ease with those in
the Commission. On March 19th a second inquiry was received
by the Commission regarding the admission of 'such persons to
be members of the Committee of Estates, who are now debarred
from public trust, they being such as have satisfied the Kirk for
the offences for which they were excluded, and are since admitted
to enter into Covenant with us'.[36] The Commission, pleading that
its attendance was too small, did not give an answer. On April 5th
the Estates requested a meeting of the Commission at Perth on
the 17th of the same month, to give 'their clear and deliberate
judgement and resolution if it be sinful and unlawful to repeal the
"Act of Classes" '.[37] The Commission, which included Rutherford,
took evasive action, declaring that it could not meet on the date
stated. The Synod, meeting at Cupar, strongly urged that the matter
should be resolved, Parliament being counselled to go ahead with
the proposed repeal. Rutherford, along with others, strongly
objected. A letter was sent from the Synod to the Commons
expressing its approval, noting the dissent of Rutherford and his
fellow objectors, disapproval for which they were cited before
the General Assembly.[38]

On May 24th, the Commission passed the controversial issue of Engagers on to the Commons, justifiably so, considering the Commission did not pass the Act of Classes, and could not repeal it. The Commission, however, did not hand over the matter to the Commons without conditions. It laid down four:

1. No Act of Parliament dealing with religion since 1648 to be repealed.
2. No revenge to be executed against anti-Engagers.
3. No anti-Engagers to be removed from office, nor any who were still trustworthy though placed since 1648.
4. Any received again by Parliament to subscribe to the Covenants.

That same day the Commission sent a letter to the presbyteries pressing them to coerce anti-Resolutioners, with the threat of bringing them before the Assembly. Baillie noted that 'Mr. S. Rutherford and Mr. James Guthrie wrote peremptory letters to the old way',[39] action which Rutherford and Guthrie continued to take until the Assembly met in St. Andrews on July 16th.

In this Assembly the leadership of the Protester party fell to Rutherford. Warriston, who might have become leader, was too afraid of the Committee of Estates to attend, while Patrick Gillespie and James Guthrie, two other possible leaders, were hardly in a position to exercise much influence, by reason of their insecurity as members. The Resolutioners were grieved to see Rutherford in the opposing camp. He was associated with Westminster and the triumph of Presbyterianism, his efforts being largely responsible for it. They knew that many would follow where Rutherford led. They blamed Warriston for the opposition of Rutherford. Warriston recorded in his diary that Rutherford was 'ensnared by others'.[40]

The anti-Resolution party not only schemed for at least the postponement of and at best the refusal of the ratification of the Resolution, they also objected to members of the Commons, who passed the Resolution, taking their seats, maintaining that the Commons' proceedings were scandalous.

Rutherford submitted a paper criticising the constitution of the

Assembly, which after fierce debates was set aside and condemned
as subversive.[41] Rutherford declared that the Assembly was
unlawful on four counts:

1. It was, so Rutherford maintained, a pre-limited Assembly,
   the freedom to choose commissioners being impeded by
   the Commissioners' letter to the presbyteries, requesting
   them to name all unsatisfied men to the Assembly, if after
   conference they were still not satisfied.
2. He believed that the King's letter overawed the Assembly.
3. The Lord High Commissioner's speech had the effect of
   prelimiting the members of the Assembly.
4. Members of the preceding Commission of Assembly, which
   had led to defection, were members of the Assembly.[42]

Rutherford had the support of Warriston. The latter recorded
in his diary[43] how Rutherford handed in his papers to the Assembly.
Rutherford also handed to the Moderator Warriston's public letter
of protest against the Resolutioners. Although a promise was made
that it would be read on July 18th or 19th, it was never read.[44] It is
surprising that, in view of Rutherford's strong criticism of the
constitution, the Assembly took no action against him, especially
when, after its removal to Dundee, it deposed Gillespie, Guthrie
and Simpson. The Commission which met at Alyth on 28th August
would have deposed him, had it not been captured by the English
forces.[45] The Assembly became definitely anti-Protester and issued
what was called 'A warning and declaration directed against
Protesters'. Rutherford was their spokesman in reply.[46] Rutherford
found himself leader of the Protester party, assisted by Gillespie
and Guthrie, in spite of the fact that he did not sympathise with
the political scheming of Gillespie, Guthrie and Warriston. The
Protesters considered themselves fortunate that they had the
services of Rutherford. The party drew its support mainly from
the ranks of the anti-Engagers and the ultra-puritanical party.
Despite Rutherford's Westminster image and ability to lead, there
was never the unity and solidarity that characterised the
Presbyterian cause in the English capital.

The Resolutioners were led by David Dickson and Robert

Douglas. They were able to count on the support of the Estates until Charles' defeat at Worcester. Baillie would have us believe that the Protester cause was widely embraced among the younger ministers,[47] many of whom had been Remonstrants. Rutherford never adopted a cause without labouring zealously for it. Warriston in his diary portrays him during August 1651, busy with his pen, writing papers, letters and sermons on behalf of the Protesters. Rutherford's defence of his Protesting zeal is clearly expressed in a letter to a Glasgow minister, whom Wodrow believes was probably despised by the Resolutioners, or had in some way suffered at their hands.[48] Possibly, the minister was Patrick Gillespie, whom we have noted was deposed at Dundee. 'Though you seem to be a man of strife and contention,' Rutherford wrote to him, 'yet you are no otherways for strife and contention than your Master before you, who came not to find peace, but rather division and contention with the malignant party.'[49] Rutherford himself was considered a man of strife and contention, even by his erstwhile friends. If he was guilty of these sins, then it was because conscience directed, and circumstances dictated.

The defeat of Charles at Worcester complicated the situation for all but die-hard Royalists in Scotland. The Protesters met in Edinburgh at the beginning of October 1651 to take stock of their position and formulate a common policy. Rutherford, the acknowledged leader, acted as Moderator. Although it began in the atmosphere of a confessional, with the confession of private sins, Gillespie roused the gathering to a vigorous prosecution of the Protestations. Protesters were in no mood for compromise. It is not surprising, therefore, that Charles, Public Resolutions and the St. Andrews Assembly were all condemned. The St. Andrews Assembly was declared invalid and the Committee of 1650 deemed to be still in existence.

A further turn in events came in December of 1651 when western Protesters gathered in Kilmarnock and produced a pamphlet entitled *A discovery after some search of the sins of the Ministers*. Balfour, in his *Annals*,[50] informs us that Guthrie and Gillespie were responsible, but the influence of Rutherford can be seen in resistance to monarchy, maintenance of the privilege of Parliament, and the defence of Presbyterial government. Not all Protesters took such a rigid line as Rutherford. Some were ready and willing to come to terms with Cromwell. A Protesters' 'Commission' meeting in Edinburgh debated the party's attitude to Cromwell. It was a far from peaceful gathering. Many of the laity, tired of ministerial dictation, advocated coming to terms with the Protector. The outcome of the turbulent assembly was the despatch of a letter to Cromwell, the object of which was, it seems, to curry favour with the Protector. If such was the case, then the attempt misfired; Cromwell showed little interest in it. By the beginning of 1654, the divisions among the Protesters were obvious to all, and damaging to their cause. An attempt in February of that year to heal their divisions was justified. Alas, the attempt failed. It was thought that Warriston and Gillespie had made overtures to Cromwell.

Since it proved impossible to bring unity to the ranks of the Protesters, it was unlikely that Protester and Resolutioner could be reconciled. An attempt, however, was made. Ministers from the opposing parties met in Edinburgh in May, 1652. Warriston persuaded Rutherford not to attend. Rutherford had no stomach for reconciliation. He, at this time, was becoming increasingly disillusioned with his party, because of its failure to adopt a firm non-compromising stance. During the winter of 1652, the Protesters lost the support of the puritan extremists, such as Menzies, Charteris, and Jaffray, Provost of Aberdeen. In October, many of the Westlanders joined the ranks of the Resolutioners. In November a further attempt was made to reconcile the two opposing parties, but alas, the effort was in vain, largely because of the Protesters' publication of the papers entitled *Nullity of the Dundee Assembly* and *Causes of God's Wrath*. Rutherford was firm in his refusal to come to terms with Cromwell. According to Rutherford, those who advocated compromise with the Protector were traitors to the Protester cause. Rutherford defended his anti-Cromwell stand in his *Testimony against English Actings in Scotland*, a work in which he was assisted by Guthrie. The *coup de grâce* for the Protesters was administered by Cromwell's troops, when on 20th July, 1653, Colonel Cotterel dissolved the rival

Resolutioner and Protester Assemblies which had been meeting in St. Giles' Church in Edinburgh, separated only by a wooden partition. By the time this happened Rutherford was out of sympathy with the Protester party, contenting himself with the work of the pen in writing the *Covenant of Life* and *The Influences of the Life of Grace*.

The Cromwellian administration of Scotland was most unpopular. Baillie complained of the poverty of the country and the crushing burden of taxation.[51] Rutherford was ever a bitter opponent of the Protector. When Cromwell attempted to regulate the settlement of ministers, Rutherford made a strong attack upon sectaries and toleration. Gillespie's Ordinance of 8th May, 1654,* was met with an outcry, when it arrived from London. Row, in his *Life of Blair*, commented: 'All those whose names were in it, except some Protesters, did speak much against it and condemned it.'[52] Monck* was quick to sense Scottish opposition to the Ordinance. In a letter to the Protector he wrote: 'The Ministers here, most of whome (as well Remonstrators as others) are very much dissatisfied with the Instruccions brought downe by Mr. Galeaspie, and very few if any will act in it, but I perceive they do rather incline to declare against it.'[53] Rutherford expressed his condemnation at a specially convened meeting in Warriston's house.[54] Cromwell was well content to see the political power of the Church of Scotland weakened by internal division. The partisan jockeying for his favour put him in a most advantageous position, although he had a great deal of sympathy with the Protesters. He even went so far as to send by letter for Robert Blair, Robert Douglas and James Guthrie to discuss 'the discomposed condician both of the godly people and ministers of Scotland'. None of the three in fact accepted the invitation. Blair excused himself on health grounds; Guthrie, in a letter, expressed his peremptoriness not to go, and Douglas, with Monck's influence, was excused.[55]

---

* Patrick Gillespie and his party received a commission from Cromwell to settle the affairs of the Church in terms of an Ordinance dated 8th May, 1654.

* George Monck, 1st Duke of Albemarle, (1608-70), administered Scotland during Cromwell's Protectorate.

Rutherford, who fell into the category of a 'rigid Presbyterian gentleman' as a News Letter from Scotland to Major General Lambert described opponents of the Commonwealth, denied Cromwell the luxury of ruling through the Protesters. Monck also favoured co-operation with the Protesters, but for a better reason than that advanced by Warriston, namely that the Resolutioners had ceased to pray for Charles because of Broghill's intervention* rather than his own request.[56] Monck, too, like Cromwell, saw that whatever his own disposition, partisan strife within the national church of Scotland was to his advantage, rather than the establishment of unity among ministers which the Ordinance was designed to advance.[57] Monck viewed assemblies of ministers as dangerous. His order book contains a warrant to a Lieutenant Colonel Gough commanding him to go to a meeting place of ministers informing them that they disperse from the town within six hours after the warning.[58] The Ordinance, however, far from uniting the ministers further divided them. Cromwell had hoped to come to an understanding with the leaders of the Remonstrants, sending for Gillespie and two others in March, 1654,[59] but to them he was a usurper. Their reply to the Ordinance expressed in two publications entitled *Considerations* and *Grievances* was clear. Indeed if there was one thing in which Protesters and Resolutioners were agreed upon, it was their opposition to Cromwell.

Yet for all its divisiveness the Ordinance did bring moderates together. James Dickson and Robert Blair convened a meeting in Edinburgh to bring together the opposing parties in June 1655 – a meeting from which Rutherford was absent. Gillespie welcomed their proposals, possibly with an eye to currying further favour in Commonwealth circles. Warriston and Guthrie, ever stalwarts of the Protester cause, rejected any suggestion of union, unless there was a thorough purge of the church, a move which would have led to the dominance of the Protesters. Baillie informs us that the insistence of Warriston and Guthrie brought about the breakdown of the meeting.[60] It was providential that Rutherford did not attend.

---

* Lord Broghill, President of the Council of Eight constituted in Edinburgh in 1655, which sought to persuade Resolutioners and Protesters to live peacefully under Cromwell's government.

He was totally opposed to Gillespie's pandering to the Protector, and having no sympathy with the obstinacy of Guthrie and Warriston, if present, he would have been forced to plough a lone furrow.

The meeting at least made it clear that the issues between the Protesters and Resolutioners could not be resolved by any human initiative; only time and changed circumstances could heal the breach. This is precisely what happened. The meeting to all intents and purposes marks the end of the division as a dominating factor in Scottish religious history. After 1656 Guthrie and Warriston gradually moved towards Cromwell, Guthrie eventually accepting a post in the Protectorate. Warriston and Guthrie, still obsessed by the idea of a covenant, pled for a new one. Baillie reported that Guthrie 'put the idea before a meeting of Protesters in January, 1655.'[61] Gillespie, eager to please Cromwell, rejected it, fearing it would incur the Protector's displeasure. Guthrie, undeterred, busied himself with its drafting, completing it by September of that year. Unfortunately no copy of Guthrie's draft is extant.

The Scottish Council, highly incensed by Guthrie and Warriston's defection to Cromwell, issued a summons for them to appear before it. They were fortunate in escaping with no greater embarrassment than an apology. The covenant project failed; even in the Covenanting west of the country there was disapproval of it. The move to place power in the hands of the Protesters had manifestly proved unsuccessful. The Resolutioners, to the delight of their opponents, also incurred the displeasure of the Protectorate, largely because of their insistence upon praying for the young Charles. In spite of declarations against this practice on August 2nd, 1652, and March 26th, 1655, prayers continued to be said, resulting in the imprisonment of many.

Fortunately, in divided Scotland, there were still those eager to reconcile the opposing parties, a further attempt being made in 1655. Gillespie arranged a meeting of Edinburgh ministers that, in Baillie's words, 'it might be seen by whose fault the discord continued'.[62] The conference was convened on November 8th, 1655, and continued for three weeks. While the Resolutioners spake as one man, the Protesters were divided into three groups.

Some advocated union with their opponents, while others stood by the Ordinance, a third party being determined to adhere to the Protestation. It is to the credit of both Resolutioners and Protesters that the breach was almost healed. Warriston and Guthrie, as strongly as ever opposed to the reconciliation with the Resolutioners, had the satisfaction of seeing the conference close with both parties still at odds. Rutherford, wearied with the bickering of both sides, did not attend. Warriston's conduct is difficult to explain. Along with Broghill he sought to form a group that favoured friendship with Cromwell, but for all his Cromwellian sympathy, he declined to hold office under the Protector, even though he was badly in need of remuneration. However, he bitterly regretted that the post of Lord Clerk Register, which could have been his, was offered to James Simpson, a candidate whom Rutherford supported with a commendatory letter.

Cromwell's policy of *divide et impera* roused religious animosity among the Scots. This suited the Protector well, although he favoured the Protesters. They requested a Commission to govern the Church according to laws on the statute book before 1651, and the establishment of a Committee of Visitation, within each synod, supervised by a general committee selected from the synods. Rutherford opposed this proposition. When first established during the Civil War, it was an Erastian move, dangerous to Presbyterianism. Rutherford was justified in his opposition to the Commission, since, although responsible to the Assembly, it created an oligarchy, with the synodical committee forming a bureaucracy hitherto unknown in Presbyterianism. The Church was in danger of surrendering its spiritual independency to the State. Erastianism, so strongly condemned in former years, was advocated as an expedient by those who should have resisted it.

Cromwell had every reason to doubt the ability of the Scottish Church to reform itself.[63] By 1657 it was obvious, even to the most rabid Protesters, that their cause had little hope of success. The Protesters had missed the opportunity of becoming the dominant party within the Church. The rejection of a petition by Guthrie to the Council, requesting the replacement of a Resolutioner minister in Stirling by a Protester, was turned down.

This, along with the news that Warriston had at last accepted office in the Protectorate, sounded the death knell of the Protesters' cause. It appeared too that England was drifting towards monarchy, Cromwell becoming king under the terms of the 'Humble Petition and Advice', a turn of events which called forth the republication of Rutherford's *Lex Rex* under the title *Treatise of Civil Polity*.

While Rutherford was disillusioned with the Protester party by reason of its divisions and the self-seeking of some of its leaders, he had no sympathy with the Resolutioners. To him they were covenant breakers, many of whom were guilty of consorting with Malignants. The Resolutioners were highly incensed by the publication of Rutherford's *Survey of the Survey*, a treatise on Thomas Hooker's views as to church discipline. A meeting of presbytery correspondents in Edinburgh on 25th May, 1658, called for a revision of it by ministers and professors.[64] Resolutioners took particular exception to Rutherford's approval of Hooker's assertions that inferior courts should not acquiesce in the findings of a superior court. Rutherford maintained that courts censuring the Protesters had done so arbitrarily.

Rutherford's Latter Days

After 1658, Rutherford rapidly receded from the public eye. He was not involved in the political manoeuvring which took place between Cromwell's death and the Restoration in 1660. He never trusted Sharp,* and when the Resolutioners sent Sharp to London in November 1658 to counter the counsels of Warriston and Argyll, in the debate on the Bill of Union, it served to justify both his low regard for Sharp and his antagonism to the Resolutioners. Before the business of the Bill could be completed, Richard Cromwell's Parliament was dissolved on 21st April, 1659. It was succeeded by the restored Rump, an assembly that had no ear for Sharp. The wheel of fortune had turned for Warriston. He found himself a

---

* James Sharp (1613-79), minister of Crail in Fife, sent as an envoy of the Resolutioners to Cromwell in August 1656. After the Restoration of Charles II in 1660 he was made Archbishop of St Andrews and became a persecutor of the Covenanters. He was assassinated by a group of Covenanters on 3rd May, 1679.

member of the new Council of State, before which Sharp was arraigned, under the suspicion of communicating with Charles.

Sharp was sentenced to be sent back to Scotland, being ordered not to be involved in politics. He returned north on 29th April.[65] In Scotland, Sharp found an unexpected ally in Monck, who suddenly turned from the Protesters. Monck found in Sharp a useful collaborator in drawing up his declaration to the Army at Coldstream, rewarding him by taking him south to London as his adviser. Sharp served Monck well, supporting him in his restoration of the Long Parliament, which freed Scottish political prisoners detained in the Tower and sanctioned the Westminster Confession, purged of its offensive chapters. When the Long Parliament was dissolved in March, 1660, Sharp returned to Scotland with the knowledge that he had played a prominent part in preparing the way for the Restoration.

The Restoration inevitably brought about division among the Scots. Some, like Guthrie, were opposed to any kind of monarchy. Many Protesters, however, who still clung tenaciously to the concept of a covenanted king, were prepared to accept such. In this they had the support of the Resolutioners and union between them seemed possible on this ground, in spite of the years of antagonism, but Rutherford confessed that he was very sceptical as to the possibility of any union between these long opposing parties.[66]

Although the wheels ground slowly in Scotland, events occurred rapidly in London. Monck drew up the list of a select Committee, which included Sharp, Crawford and Lauderdale, Sharp being chosen as one of the deputation which in May visited Charles in Breda. By this time it was obvious even to obdurate Protesters that Episcopacy would probably be restored. They were greatly perturbed by the swift movement of events, and called upon Douglas to petition the king against any such action. Douglas not only refused to lend his support to them, but he warned the Protesters that their day was almost at an end, and that they could not count upon the ear of the king.[67] The timeliness of Douglas' warning was proved by the arrests of Argyll, Sir James Stewart and Sir John Chiesley. Warriston escaped, only to be arrested later and then executed. Guthrie and other Protesters were arrested at a meeting in Edinburgh on 23rd August.

On the last day of that month, Sharp returned from London bearing a letter from Charles to the Presbytery of Edinburgh in which he promised to preserve the government of the Church of Scotland, recognise the Acts of Resolutioner Assemblies, and summon a further Assembly. The promises proved to be worthless. No Assembly was called; Parliament, meeting on New Year's Day 1661, removed all the Covenanting legislation from the Statute Book. Accordingly it was no surprise that Episcopacy was restored on 6th September.

During the last two years of the Commonwealth period, Rutherford, restrained by sickness and advancing years, kept within the confines of St. Andrews, expressing opinions to presbyteries only when consulted. St. Andrews was not an amenable atmosphere in which Rutherford could work. M'Ward described it as 'the very nursery of all superstition in worship, and error in doctrine and the sack of all profanity in conversation among students'.[68] Certainly the staff of the college had accepted the Covenant, but some who had been appointed to their posts by the Primate, Dr. Barron, because he openly favoured Episcopacy, were forced to resign. The Principal, Dr. Howie, who had voiced his allegiance to the Covenant, retained his post which he had held since 1608, until he was succeeded by Rutherford in 1647. On becoming Principal, Rutherford found that his energy was absorbed by administrative work, rectifying errors made in the payment of college rents, the result of mismanagement by Howie. This would have lost Howie his post as Principal. Long before, indeed, he had offered to resign, but the intervention of Henderson, his former university colleague, enabled him to continue.

There is evidence that Rutherford was Rector of the University in 1643.[69] Murray, in his biography,[70] states that he held this position in 1651, which according to Baillie[71] became the responsibility of James Wood in 1655. We find Rutherford as one of the Commission which met in Edinburgh in 1648 to plan a uniform system of teaching.[72] His selection was justified: Rutherford was an educationalist as well as theologian. Students, however, were divided as to his ability to impart knowledge. McLeod in his

Scottish Theology[73] repeated that 'Rutherford was confused in his notions and methods of teaching, applying himself to the writing of books against the sectaries'. Until Alexander Colville was recalled from Sidon to assist in 1642, administration and teaching were the responsibility of Rutherford. Rutherford's absence at Westminster necessitated the appointment of James Wood, minister of Denino, as Professor in June, 1645.

Inevitably the divisions in the Presbyterian ranks found their way into the college. Staff and students took sides, although until the publication of the Public Resolutions harmony prevailed. Wood and Colville were Resolutioners. Wood, unhappy with the division among students and staff, requested removal (a request that was granted), becoming Principal of St. Leonard's. Rutherford's nomination of William Rait as his successor was rejected in favour of Colville's suggestion that James Sharp be appointed, an appointment that could bring nothing but sorrow to Rutherford.

Rutherford's vociferous support for the Protesters' cause alienated many of his former friends. His uncharitable refusal of fellowship with Blair and Wood at a communion service brought further disfavour upon him. Balfour's comment that Rutherford was the 'irreconcilable voice of mercy and charity, though a preacher of both in others'[74] seems justified. It must be said, however, to Rutherford's credit, that on his deathbed he expressed his great appreciation of Wood.

Rutherford was a lone protagonist for the Protesters' cause not only in the Presbytery of St. Andrews but also in the Synod of Fife. He would have welcomed an end to the Protester-Resolutioner division,[75] but, suspicious of his opponents, disillusioned with the leaders of his own party and loyal to his former companions, reconciliation was impossible.

The arrest and imprisonment of Guthrie after penning a petition to the king, reminding him of his obligation to the Covenant, foreshadowed the fate of Rutherford.[76] Rutherford penned his own petition, directed to his comrades in the south-west. In it he professed his eagerness to congratulate Charles upon his accession to the throne, but expressed his fear of both popery and prelacy on the one hand, and sectarianism on the other. A letter to a fellow minister written from St. Andrews, in the same year as the Restoration, explained why Rutherford refused to petition the Committee of Estates for the release of Guthrie and others imprisoned with him in Edinburgh castle. His principal reason was that a petition would compromise the Covenant, something unthinkable to Rutherford.[77] Rutherford's insistence upon the Covenant made him a marked man.

Guthrie and his fellow prisoners were released, but Rutherford's *Lex Rex* was condemned by the Committee of Estates on September 15th, all copies to be handed to the Crown Solicitor before October 16th. On the latter date some copies were publicly burned in Edinburgh by the hangman, and a week later copies of Rutherford's work met with a similar fate at the gate of his own college in St. Andrews and in London. Rutherford was stripped of all the posts he held, including his pastoral charge, his stipend being confiscated. He was called upon to appear before the Committee of Estates on a charge of treason.

Rutherford's letter to Guthrie, dated February 15th, 1661, reveals a mind ready for martyrdom. He would have welcomed such, and indeed would have died the death of a martyr if ill health had not prevented his appearance in the winter of 1660. In March, 1661, he was again cited by Parliament to appear. When it was obvious that death would cheat his enemies of their prey, Parliament was not prepared to allow him to die in college. But Lord Burleigh protested: 'Ye have voted that honest man out of his college,' he said, 'but ye cannot vote him out of heaven.' Rutherford died on March 29th, 1661, his last words being addressed to his wife, who survived him by fourteen years. He was buried in the churchyard of the chapel of St. Regulus in St. Andrews. Such was the esteem in which he was held, and the veneration accorded to him, that for some time after his death many requested to be buried near to his mortal remains.

CHAPTER 7

THE MAN OF EXTREMES

It remains in this final chapter to make an estimate of Rutherford's life and character. What kind of man was Rutherford? Was he a mystic who more than most men enjoyed the intimacy of life with Christ? Was he a democrat or autocrat where ecclesiastical issues were concerned? Was he a valiant defender of the Covenant or was he its bigoted protagonist? It is not surprising that he should present a problem to us, for he was an enigma to himself. To David Dickson he wrote, 'I am made of extremes.'[1] To the same correspondent, one of his closest friends, he complained, 'I fear that ye have never known me well. If ye saw my inner side, it is possible that ye would pity me, but you would hardly give me either love or respect: men mistake me the whole length of the heavens.'[2] It is understandable that Rutherford should complain of being misunderstood and misinterpreted by his contemporaries. His silence concerning the scandal of his early days leaves him open to the accusations of his detractors. At a distance of over three centuries we are forced to conjecture why it was that he resigned his post as Professor of Humanity at Edinburgh. We cannot expect an unbiased judgement from an Episcopalian or English Independent. Even if the anecdote of Archbishop Ussher's visit to the manse at Anwoth is not apocryphal, it expresses no more than the prelate's respect for Rutherford as a preacher.

If Rutherford testified to the saintliness of the lives of 'Independent' Divisions he met at Westminster, his assault upon their ecclesiastical position in the Assembly, and his criticism of their doctrines on paper did not endear the name of Rutherford to seventeenth century Independency. Nor can we expect any Resolutioner, not even as close a friend as Dickson, to see Rutherford without prejudice. Biographers like Thomson have tended to romanticise Rutherford's ministry at Anwoth, and we are dependent on Rutherford himself in giving an account of the confinement in Aberdeen. It is at the time of the Westminster Assembly that testimony is given to Rutherford's character, 'the clearness of intellect, warmth and earnestness of affection and loftiness and spirituality of devotional feeling,'[3] as well as his ability as a theologian and debater, which Baillie described as 'the great parts God has given him'.[4] It is difficult to believe that the man who penned the *Letters* is the author of *Lex Rex*, or the preacher of the homely sermons of Anwoth is the Westminster Divine. It is unjust to pass facile judgements upon Rutherford on the ground of some particular action, such as his refusal to share the Table with Blair at St. Andrews, or some attitude taken, such as his fanatical adherence to the Protesters' cause. If we are to attempt an estimate of his life and character then we must take a comprehensive view of him. We must see him as the dedicated pastor of Anwoth as well as the learned Divine of Westminster, and the fierce controversialist of St. Andrews. To condemn him as vindictive, unmerciful and uncharitable is manifestly unjust.

Was Rutherford a Mystic?

To Taylor Innes, Rutherford was a mystic,[5] but Rutherford would not have agreed. In his *Covenant of Life*[6] he asserted that 'truth cannot be gained mystically, a man may be very God, yet stumble'. Rufus Jones[7] had no hesitation in categorically stating that Rutherford was a bitter opponent of mysticism. If Rutherford is to be considered a mystic, then it must be admitted that his mysticism has to be distinguished from that of the Familists and the Theologia Germanica.* To the Familists, union was fusion or identity with Christ, while for the Theologica Germanica mysticism was the identification of soul as the very essence of God. In his *Survey of the Spiritual Anti-Christ*, Rutherford strongly objected to such Familist teaching that believers are 'Godded' and 'Christed' with the being of God in faith and love.[8]

---

* The Familists were members of a sect called the 'Family of Love' founded by Henry Nicholas, which held vaguely pantheistic views. The 'Theologia Germanica' was a late-fourteenth century mystical treatise. Both offered ways by which the soul could be absorbed into the being of God.

For Rutherford union with Christ was spiritual marriage. Therefore he expressed Christian experience in marital terms. Rutherford's imagery is certainly sensuous. Nothing apparently could be more erotic than his statement that 'I confidently believe there is a bed made for Christ and me, and that we shall take our fill of love in it',[9] or his words to David Dickson, 'Sometimes when I have Christ in my arms I fall asleep in the sweetness of His presence, and He in my sleep stealeth away out of my arms, and when I awake, I miss Him.'[10] In Rutherford's writings the Bride is variously identified. Sometimes she is an individual, as in his letters to Lady Kenmure after the death of her husband,[11] and to Jean Brown, mother of the minister of Wamphray, to whom he commended Christ as her 'last living and longest living husband, – the staff of her old age'.[12] On other occasions the 'Bride' was identified as the Church. Such was the case in a missive to Marion McNaught at the time of the threatened introduction of the service book, where he wrote of Christ as 'Our dead husband – wooing His kirk'. Such was the case too in a letter to Lady Kenmure, when he expressed the fear that the kirk was 'going to Rome's brothel house to seek a lover of her own' and had 'given up with Christ as her husband'.[13] For Rutherford, the Bride could be a single congregation. In a letter to his parishioners, he exclaimed, 'What could I want if my ministry among you should make a marriage between the little bride in these bounds and the bridegroom.'[14] Further, on occasions the Bride was his beloved Scotland. He complained to Lady Kenmure that a 'false and declining Scotland, whom our Lord took off the dunghill and out of hell and made a fair bride to Himself hath broken her faith to her sweet husband, and hath put on the forehead of a whore'.[15] We must not deduce too much from Rutherford's erotic language, since he was steeped in that of the Canticles and could hardly avoid marital imagery. Although not a mystic he employed mystical language. Spiritual life for him was a romance; his concept of union was that of spiritual sympathy.

This is made clear in a letter to Lady Kenmure, prior to her removal to England: 'I trust ye are so betrothed in marriage to the true Christ, that you will not give your love to any false Christ. Ye know not how soon your marriage day will come; nay is not eternity hard upon you,' he wrote.[16] It is even more marked in a letter he wrote to the same Lady, on the death of Lord Kenmure. 'Your dearest Lord made you a widow woman for Christ, who is now suiting for marriage love of you. And therefore since you lie alone in your bed, let Christ be as a bundle of myrrh, to sleep and lie all the night, betwixt your breasts and then your bed is better filled than before.'[17]

The psychologist Leuba in his *Psychology of Religious Mysticism* has made much of the mystic's relations with the opposite sex. Rutherford's *Letters* give ample evidence of close if not intimate friendships with women, especially Marion McNaught. There was such an affinity of spirit between Rutherford and Marion McNaught, whom he described as 'a woman to whom Jesus is dearer than her own heart',[18] that their association was bound to be close. 'Rutherford is not surely to be blamed for loving such a hearer,' wrote Alexander Whyte. 'When two fanatics so full of humour as Samuel Rutherford and Marion McNaught met they corresponded ever after with one another in their own enraptured language night and day.'[19]

From the scandal of his early years, and the many warnings he gave against youthful lusts, we may conclude that Rutherford was strongly sexed, but further we cannot go. There is no evidence of an *affaire d'amour* with Marion McNaught, nor any other of his female correspondents. The intimacy they enjoyed was that of the pen.

Is not the answer to the question of Rutherford's mysticism to be found, at least partly, in his remarkable spiritual growth? On 1st January, 1637, he wrote, 'I profess I have never taken pains to find out Him whom my soul loveth, there is a gate of finding out Christ that I have never lightened upon.'[20] By that year he seems to have reached a level of elation; he repeatedly refers to having arrived at a particular 'nick' in Christianity. 'I verily think now that Christ hath led me up to a nick in Christianity that I was never at before,' he wrote to Alexander Gordon. 'I think all before was but childhood and bairns play.'[21] Three days later he wrote in similar vein to Alexander Colville of Blair: 'He hath led me up to such a pitch and nick of joyful communion with Himself, as I never knew before. When I look back to bygones I judge myself to have been a child at A, B, C with Christ.'[22] Further, on the following day he wrote to Earlston the Younger: 'I behoved to come to Aberdeen to learn a new mystery in Christ – nay verily I was a child before, all bygones are but bairns play – I have heard and seen this in his sweetness, so as I am almost saying, it is not He that I was want to meet with. He smileth more cheerfully, His kisses are more sweet and soul refreshing than the kisses of the Christ I saw before were, though He be the same. Or rather the King hath led me up to a measure of joy and communion with my Bridegroom that I never attained to before.'[23] To David Dickson he witnessed to the same elation: 'It is not jest nor sport which maketh me to speak and write as I do: I never before came to that nick or pitch of communion with Christ that I have attained to.'[24] It is evident that Rutherford had a strong sense of the awareness of the presence of God. Having reached such a state of ecstasy, it was inevitable he should express it in the mental imagery of the Canticles, with which his soul was so steeped. Union with Christ there was, but it is not the fusion of the mystic. Certainly the marriage relationship readily comes to mind, but he wrote too in terms of horticulture, of the rose in union with the root: 'The rose is surest in being, in beauty on its own stalk, and root, and the rose keeps its first union with the root and it shall never wither, never cast its blossom or greenness of beauty.'[25] He saw himself, too, as fallow ground to be broken up and made fruitful for the Lord. 'O that this withered lea-ground,' he wrote to Robert Gordon, 'were made fertile to bear a crop for Him, by whom it is so painfully dressed.'[26]

It was his intimacy with Christ that awoke such a strong sense of sin in his sensitive soul. He regretted that he 'like a fool summoned Christ for unkindness', and complained of his 'fickleness and inconsistency'.[27] During the period of his banishment to Aberdeen he wrote, 'The devil hath a controversy in the house, and I blame upon Christ for my heart was filled with upbraidings and I feared I was an outcast, and that I was but a withered tree in the vineyard and but held the sun off the good plants with my idle shadow.'[28] There is a resemblance in Rutherford to Paul. The apostle bewailed the fact that there was nothing good in him, and cried out, 'O wretched man that I am, who shall deliver me from the body of this death?'[29] Perhaps Paul's experience is able to lead us to an understanding of Rutherford's. Paul did not seek religious emotion and ecstasy for their own sake, nor did Rutherford. For neither was Christ an intermittent, but an abiding presence. For both a sense of union with Christ came not from spiritual exercises but by revelation. There is no evidence of a pantheistic union in Rutherford any more than there was in Paul. Rutherford, for all his mystical tendencies, never lost his identity. Clearly throughout his career he is always Rutherford in and united to Christ. Patently we must conclude that Rutherford's mysticism was not the experience we usually associate with the word, not self absorption in his own individual experience, but that union with Christ which is the right of every Christian.

Autocrat or Democrat?
Rutherford's insistence upon the freedom of the local congregation to choose its own minister, even to the point that the franchise should not be limited to the heads of families alone, but should even include women, appears to be at variance with his denial of toleration to Episcopalians and sectaries. If we feel that his condemnation of prelacy betrays an absence of grace, we must remember that prelacy and its associated practices were imposed upon the Kirk in Scotland by princes and prelates who were prepared to employ physical violence to achieve their end. Those who see Charles I as a loyal Anglican and a martyr for its cause, with no intention of restoring Romanism, have the advantage of viewing him from the distance of three centuries. For Rutherford the Reformation was hardly complete, the results of secession from Rome had not been secured. Seventeenth century English Puritans and Scottish Presbyterians can hardly be blamed for suspecting a Romeward aim in Charles' insistency upon prelacy, the use of the service book and its associated ceremonies.

We readily accept the observance of Christmas and Easter as the twin foundation festivals of the Christian year, but to

Rutherford the observance of any day apart from the Sabbath was 'unlawful will worship, not warranted by God's Word'. 'No day beside the Sabbath,' he wrote to his parishioners, '(which is of His own appointment) should be kept holy and sanctified with preaching and the public worship of God, for the memory of Christ's birth, death, resurrection and ascension.'[30]

While English Free churchmen and Scottish Presbyterians witness to the prophetic nature of the ministry by wearing the Geneva gown, objecting to the use of the surplice, few would go as far as Rutherford, describing it as 'the attire of the mass priest, the garment of Baal's priest'.[31] While the majority of Free churchmen and Presbyterians prefer not to kneel for communion, few would go as far as Rutherford, condemning the practice as 'superstition and idolatry'. Rutherford's language lacks tolerance and grace, but he lived in an age of intolerance and religious strife.

Rutherford was no friend of Independency either, even though he witnessed to the godliness of the Independents, who he wrote to Lady Kenmure, 'come nearest to walkers with God'.[32] He contended with them 'that ordination of pastors belongeth not to a single congregation but to a college of presbyters', and that 'one single congregation hath not power to excommunicate'.[33] Rutherford had no hesitation in condemning Independency as 'contrary to God's Word'.[34] Anabaptists, for Rutherford, were associated with such questionable sects as Libertines and Antinomians, while the 'Seekers', akin to the present day Society of Friends, were consigned to the same category. In spite of the suffering Rutherford shared with them, Rutherford had no sympathy with those he knew as sectaries. How are we to explain his attitude to his fellow sufferers?

We must remember that in seventeenth century Scotland the issue was between Presbyterianism and Episcopacy. At the Reformation the country overthrew the Roman yoke and took its lead from Geneva. The revival of Episcopacy in Scotland came not from the grassroots of the people, but from the attempt of the Stuarts to impose it upon an unwilling nation. Presbyterianism was not contested by other religious bodies until the eighteenth century, and then with little success. In Scotland Independents

were few and far between. Robert Browne, who may be termed
'the Father of Independency', driven from England by persecution,
after visiting Flanders came to Scotland in 1583, landing at
Dundee. He was arraigned before the Edinburgh presbytery on
January 20th, 1584, but the King appears to have looked kindly
upon his bold defiance of the Kirk and shielded him from further
persecution. Although Browne travelled far and wide throughout
Scotland, he does not seem to have left behind him any Independent
churches. In 1589, Browne was followed by another stalwart of
the Independents, Penry, who was to become a martyr for their
cause, being executed at Tyburn in 1593. Like Browne, he did not
leave behind him any Independent churches in Scotland. Since
Browne had hardly endeared himself to the Scottish Presbyterians,
and no movement in favour of Independency had been initiated
either by Penry or him, the Scots were content that it remained in
England and prayed it would never gain a foothold in Scotland.

The General Assembly took steps to this end. The earliest direct
declaration of the General Assembly against Independency is to
be found in a letter to some ministers in England, who were alarmed
at the incursion of Independency into Presbyterian churches south
of the border. An Act of the Assembly in 1647, expressing the
fear that Independency would find its way into Scotland, was the
first of several. Presbyterian objections to Independency were
twofold, the freedom of the local congregation from presbyterial
control and liberty of conscience. As we have seen Rutherford
campaigned for the right of the local congregation to elect its own
minister, and allow certain powers of censure and government in
particular congregations,[35] but further he would not go. As a
protagonist of Presbyterianism, he maintained it was the right of
presbytery to ordain and induct. As for liberty of conscience, he
insisted upon a national conformity, imposed if necessary by the
power of the civil magistrate, a thesis he strongly presented in his
Against the Pretended Liberty of Conscience. If liberty of
conscience meant that every man could do whatever he thought
right in his own eyes, then Rutherford would have none of it.

Cromwell's advocacy of Independency did not enhance its
prospects in Scotland, although some men, such as Alexander

Jaffray, provost of Aberdeen, were influenced in its direction.[36] Some, though summoned before the Synod of Aberdeen, separated themselves from the Church of Scotland in 1652.

Independent insistence upon a gathered church, with freedom for the local congregation to conduct its own affairs, was repugnant to Rutherford. He could hardly be expected to view Independency with indifference. To him, as to his fellow Presbyterians, it was 'a gangrene'.[37] The Familists, under the leadership of Henry Nichols (or Nicholas), deemed the written Word a dead letter, setting up their own conceits and fancies under the notion of Spirit; against whom Rutherford seasonably and successfully campaigned. For Rutherford the Reformed Church of his country was the establishment. His suffering came not so much from the civil power as from the prelates. The multiplicity of divisions among the English Puritans shocked and alarmed him. From Westminster he wrote, 'There is nothing here but divisions in the church and Assembly; for beside Brownists and Independents – there are many other sects here.'[38]

Rutherford maintained that the sectaries put conscience in the place of the Word. Gilmour wrote that this in practice meant giving 'man a liberty of unlimited error'.[39] To Rutherford, conscience was far too subjective a guide, since conscience, even when enlightened and activated by the Holy Spirit, is such a delicate mechanism. It is subjected to social pressures, and may well be fashioned by the thought and feeling of the age to which it belongs. It can so easily be seared or silenced. Rutherford was justified in maintaining that it was no infallible guide. He held that it is the business of the Church to interpret the Word and to act as a guide for conscience. This, of course, did not mean that Rutherford believed in an infallible church. Such a doctrine for him was a Romish fabrication. To the English Independent, liberty of conscience was a means of establishing a truly Reformed Protestant Church, free from all traces of Popery.

History has shown that liberty of conscience is an extremely dangerous weapon, in that it can be employed indiscriminately against friend as well as foe. This is precisely what happened in England. Independency covered a wide range of opinion. Some were quite willing to retain a parochial system, while others insisted on a 'gathered church', some even went so far as to believe there was a place for the civil magistrate as a nursing father to the Church, and to exercise a defensive power for religion both at home and abroad. Those who urged a greater freedom were averse to granting toleration to atheists, Socinians, Roman Catholics and extreme sects, such as Fifth Monarchists and Ranters. The intolerance of those who demanded liberty of conscience for themselves was even more evident in the newly established states of North America. As H.A.L. Fisher pointed out, 'The Puritan founders were not, and never pretended to be, the advocates of universal toleration. At that time no political community existed in which religious liberty was recognised, and it was no part of the Puritans to frame one.'[40] The Puritans of Massachusetts had no love for the Quaker immigrants. A law passed by the General Court of the colony in 1657 described them as the 'cursed sect of heretics, lately risen up in the World, who take upon them to be immediately sent of God, and infallibly assisted by the Spirit to write and speak blasphemous opinions, despising government and the order of God in church and commonwealth, speaking evil of dignities, reproaching and reviling magistrates and ministers, seeking to turn the people from the faith, and gain proselytes to their pernicious ways'. Laws were passed forbidding banished Quakers returning to the colony. However, in spite of adverse legislation, Quakers returned and several of them were hanged.

   In Scotland, Knox established a thoroughly reformed Protestant Church. Liberty of conscience was not a weapon in the cause of further reform, or to defend a national liberty already won. Rutherford and his fellow Protesters could argue that their aim was to preserve liberty of conscience, which the Resolutioners by their compromise with the 'Malignants' endangered, an argument which was substantiated by the Covenanting struggle which followed. The liberty of conscience, which Rutherford would have denied to the Resolutioners, proved to be a mirage. It was a liberty that ultimately led to bondage and bloodshed. Even David Dickson admitted in his dying hour that the Protesters were justified in the stand they took, and Robert Douglas confessed it would have been wiser to have sided with Rutherford, especially when he saw the road which his fellow Resolutioner James Sharp was taking. Rutherford's refusal to 'serve tables' with Blair was certainly regrettable and must be condemned, but they were days of sad divisions and animosities, when emotions ran high.

Although Rutherford insisted upon the right of the local congregation to select its own pastor, he was not averse to employing the arm of the civil magistrate in matters of religion. We have come to regard it as a highly dangerous practice, but this was not so evident in seventeenth century Scotland. Even Cromwell, a staunch 'Independent', who should have resisted the interference of the civil magistrate in affairs of the Church, was prepared to wield the sword against not merely prelatists and papists, but even those of his own persuasion, when occasion demanded. To Rutherford, Kirk and country were synonymous. In fact the General Assembly of the Church of Scotland was much more representative of the nation than Parliament. Rutherford did not and could not see the distinction between Church and State, which has ever been so fundamental a principle for the English Free Churchman. The situation is vastly different in Scotland from that which exists in England. While the sovereign is given his or her rightful place of honour in relation to the Kirk, from the beginning Knox made it clear that the pretensions of no earthly sovereign could ever in any way diminish the Crown Rights of the Redeemer. Melville had no hesitation in reminding James that he was no more than 'God's silly vassal'. For Rutherford, Scotland was Zion, its people were God's Israel. It was a noble ideal, but incapable of realisation. It is understandable that he should see the civil magistrate as a servant of God in Zion, appointed to administer God's law among his people. We have long abandoned the aim of establishing God's kingdom through the medium of the state. The ideal, however, was still cherished in Rutherford's day, and where was it more likely to be realised than in Scotland? Should not therefore 'every soul be subject unto the higher powers'? maintained Rutherford. We do an injustice to the seventeenth century divine if we judge him by any other standards than those of his own age.

There is little doubt that Rutherford will remain something of
an enigma to all who study his life and ministry. The *Letters* portray
him as a saint, but he owned himself a sinner. He was so sure of
heaven, yet in moments of depression he was beset with doubts
and misgivings. He was so heavenly-minded and yet he was so
involved in the politics of earth. He was a democrat yet an autocrat,
a man who demanded liberty of conscience for himself yet was
reluctant to grant it to others. His life and ministry is summed up
in words upon his gravestone in St. Andrews:

> For Zion's King, and Zion's cause
> And Scotland's covenant laws,
> Most constantly he did commend
> Until his time was at an end,
> Then he won to the full fruition
> Of that which he had seen in vision.

BIBLIOGRAPHY*

LETTERS OF RUTHERFORD

Joshua Redivivus, or Mr. Rutherford's Letters, divided into two parts. Printed in the year 1664. Several subsequent editions in 1671, 1675, 1692, 1709, 1724, 1738, 1761, 1765, 1783, 1796, 1802, 1809, 1818, 1821, 1824, 1825, 1830, 1834, 1836, 1846, 1848, 1857, 1863, 1867, 1875, 1891 (edited by the Rev. A. A. Bonar), 1899(selected letters edited by the Rev. A. A. Bonar), 1973.

Collections of Rutherford's letters are deposited in the National Library of Scotland, Edinburgh and in St. Andrews University Library.

SERMONS OF RUTHERFORD (in alphabetical order)

An Exhortation at a Communion to a Scots Congregation in London:
A Sermon on Song of Solomon 5:2-6. (This sermon was added to some copies of the 1727 edition of *Christ Dying and Drawing Sinners to Himself*. It is found in part but imperfectly reprinted by Bonar in 1876 and 1877. Bonar believed that it was preached at Anwoth on 5th April, 1637. This must be incorrect since Rutherford was in Aberdeen at that time. An exposition of Song of Solomon 5:3-6 appeared under the title of *The Spouse's Longing for Christ* in *Quaint Sermons* (*vide* below) of 1885, pp. 84–115 in which a few paragraphs of the first part are to be found. In *Quaint Sermons* Bonar gives the date and place as Anwoth, 5th April, 1647. This cannot be correct either, since at that time Rutherford was in London, attending the Westminster Assembly. If this was the sermon preached at the communion service referred to in a letter to M.M [Vol. 1, p. 147], then the date was 5th April, 1635.)

A Sermon preached to the Honourable House of Commons. (This was an exposition of Exodus 3:2, preached on Wednesday, January 31, 1643, at their solemn fast. It was printed by order of the House of Commons.)

A Sermon preached to the Honourable House of Lords. (This was

---

* In some of the older works in the Bibliography, 'f' is used instead of 's' to reflect the orthography of the period.

an exposition of Isaiah 8:17, preached in Westminster Abbey on Wednesday, June 25, 1645, the day of solemn and public humiliation.)

Christ and the Dove's Heavenly Salutations, with pleasant conference together. (An exposition of Song of Solomon 2:16-17, preached at Anwoth, before a communion in 1630. First printed 1725. Reprinted as *Heavenly Salutations with pleasant conferences between Christ and His People*, by John Bryce, to be sold at his shop opposite Gibson's Wynd, Saltmarket, Glasgow, 1778.)

Christ's Napkin or Glad Tidings to the People of God or Comfort afforded in the views of Death. (An exposition of Revelations 21:4-8, preached in Kirkcudbright at a communion service, May 12, 1633.)

Christ Dying and Drawing Sinners to Himself or A Survey of Our Saviour in His Soule Suffering and His Lonelyness in his death and the efficacie thereof. (An exposition of John 12:27, 33.)

The Cruel Watchmen. (An exposition of Song of Solomon 5:7-9, printed in Edinburgh for James Ormiston, in 1728. A further edition was printed in Glasgow for John Bryce in 1784. Bonar did not include it in his *Fourteen Communion Sermons*, published in 1877, believing that it was not genuine, but he included it in his *Quaint Sermons* of 1885 under the title of *The Church Seeking her Lord*.)

The Door of Salvation Opened or A loud and chirl voice from Heaven to unregenerate sinners on earth. (An exposition of 2nd Thessalonians 1:8. Preached in 1635. Printed and sold in Gibson's Close, Edinburgh, opposite the Cross, 1735.)

The Lamb's Marriage. (An exposition of Revelation 14:7-14, preached in Kirkcudbright at a communion service in 1634. Printed for Duncan Ferguson and sold by him, Edinburgh 1732. Reprinted and sold by John Bryce opposite Gibson's Wynd, Saltmarket, Glasgow, 1776.)

The Power and Prevalency of Faith and Prayer : Evidenced. (A discourse on Matthew 9:27-31. Printed in 1713.)

The Tryal and Triumph of Faith or An exposition of the History of Christ's Dispossession of the Daughter of the Woman of Canaan. (Based on Matthew 15:21-28, Mark 7:24-30. Published by Authority.)

Anwoth Sermons (An exposition of Zechariah 13:6-9. Preached in 1634.)

Two Communion Sermons. (Based on Hebrews 12:1-5 and Isaiah 49:1-4. Printed from an eighteenth century MS with an introduction by D. Hay Fleming in the Original Sucession Magazine, 1886).

NINETEENTH CENTURY COLLECTIONS OF SERMONS

1. *A Collection of Valuable Sermons At Sacramental occasions, on several Subjects and in different places, in the years 1630, 1634 and 1637.* By the eminently learned and pious Mr. Samuel Rutherford, Professor of Divinity at St. Andrews, First Edition, Glasgow. Printed by Stephen Young, Prince's Street for Hugh Shields, Nether Newton, and S.Y. and fold by them, Adam Ferguson, Dovehill, and the Booksellers. This was the first collection and edition of Rutherford's sermons. The editor in the preface writes that they are 'from an old MS; but whether taken from the author's mouth in shorthand, or copies from original notes is uncertain'. The sermons are based upon the following texts: Revelation 19:11-14, Isaiah 49:1, Zechariah 13:7, Zechariah 11:9-13, Zechariah 13:8, John 20:13-18, Luke 14:16, Song of Solomon 5:1, Hebrews 12:1, Song of Solomon 2:8-12. The final sermon being an exhortation at a communion.

2. *Twelve Communion Sermons* by Rev. Samuel Rutherford with a Preface and Notes by Rev. Andrew A. Bonar D.D., Glasgow, Charles Glass and Co., 85 Maxwell Street, 1876. In his preface Bonar states that the sermons are from notes of hearers. The sermons are based upon the following texts: Revelation 19:11-14, Zechariah 11:9-12, Zechariah 13:7-9, John 20:13-14, Zechariah 13:7-9, Song of Solomon 5:1 and 2, Luke 14:16-17, Revelation 21:4-7, Hebrews 12:1-5, Song of Solomon 2:14-17, Isaiah 49:1-4, Christ's love and Loveliness.

3. *Fourteen Communion Sermons* by Rev. Samuel Rutherford with a Preface and Notes by Rev. Andrew A. Bonar D.D., Glasgow, Charles Glass and Co., 85 Maxwell Street, 1876. The collection comprised of the twelve sermons listed above with two additional homilies based on Revelation 14:7-11 (*vide The Lamb's Marriage*) and Song of Solomon 2:8-12. The two sermons from Zechariah 13:7-9 were preached at Anwoth and printed in 1738 for Duncan Ferguson Chapman.

4. *Quaint Sermons of Samuel Rutherford*. Hitherto unpublished with a preface by the Rev. Andrew A. Bonar, D.D., London, Hodder and Stoughton, 27 Paternoster Row, 1885. These sermons form part of a MS in which are included other sermons previously unpublished. Bonar states in his preface: 'Who it was who took down the notes of these sermons at the time, and who it was that gathered all together in the volume, we do not know. One thing is certain, viz., he was a most attentive hearer and a faithful attender to the minister's preaching'.

The sermons included in this collection are based on the following texts: Isaiah 41:14-16, Luke 15:11-13, Isaiah 49:14-16, Luke 15:14-19, Hosea 8:1-3, Luke 15:20-21, John 20:9-13, Luke 15:22-23, Song of Solomon 5:3-6, Luke 15:24-28, Song of Solomon 5:7-10, Luke 15:29-32, Jeremiah 50:4-5, 2nd Corinthians 10:4-5, Jeremiah 50:4-5, Philippians 3:7-8, Luke 15:11-12, Philippians 3:8.

WORKS OF RUTHERFORD

Ane Catachisme Conteining the Soume of Christian Religion, in MITCHELL, A.F. *Catechisms of the Second Reformation*, Nisbet and Co., London, 1886.

A Free Disputation against pretended Liberty of Conscience tending To Resolve Doubts moved by Mr John Goodwin, John Baptist, Dr Jer. Taylor, the Belgick Arminians, Socinians and other Authors contending for the lawlesse Liberty or licentious Toleration of Sects and Heresies. London. Printed by R.I. for Andrew Crooke and are to be sold at his shop, at the signe of the Green Dragon, St. Paul's Church-yard MDCIL.

A Peaceable and Temperate Plea for Paul's Presbyterie in Scotland, A Modest and Brotherly Dispute of the Government of the Church of Scotland wherein Our Discipline is Demonstrated to be the True Apostolick Way of Divine Truth and the Arguments on the contrary are friendly dissolved, the grounds of Separation and Indepencie of particular Congregations, in defence of Ecclesiasticall Presbyteries, Synods and Assemblies, are examined and tryed. LONDON. Printed for John Bartlett at the guilt-Cup neare St Aufstans-gate 1642.

A Reflex (or Reflect) upon a Man's Mis-spent Life backed with Challenges. (A MS from a volume of seventeenth century MSS, once in the possession of Rob. Wodrow, which came into the hands of J. Sturrock for perusal. Privately owned by Dr J.D. Ogilvie. The Reflect consists of thoughts of Rutherford penned in Anwoth in the form of a directory, which he took with him to Aberdeen.) Printed in the Original Secession Magazine, 1925.

A Survey of the Spiritual Antichrist Opening The secrets of Familisme and Antinomianisme in the Antichristian Doctrine of John Saltmarsh, and Will. Del, the present preachers of the Army now in England, and of Robert Town, Tob Crisp, H. Denne, Eaton and others. In which is revealed the rife and spring of Antinomians, familists, Libertines, Swenck-feldians, Enthyfiafts. The minde of Luther a most professed oppofer of Antinomians is cleared, and diverse considerable points of the Law and the Gospel, of the Spirit and Letter, of the two Covenants, of the nature of free grace, exercife under temptationes, mortification, justification, sanctification are discovered. In two Parts. LONDON. Printed by J.D. and R. I. for Andrew Crooke and are to be sold at his shop at the Green-Dragon in Paul's Church-yard. 1648.

A Survey of the Survey of the Summe of Church-Difcipline Penned by Mr Tomas Hooker, Late Pastor of the Church at Hartford upon Connecticut in New England Wherein The Way of the Churches of N. England is now re-examined; Arguments in favour thereof winnowed; The Principles of that Way discussed; and the reasons of most seeming strength and nerves removed. LONDON. Printed by J. G. for Andr. Crook, at the Green Dragon in St Paul's Church-yard MDCLVIII.

A Testimony to the Work of Reformation in Britain and Ireland to which are added A Short Account of his LIFE with some of his last Words, Glasgow. Printed by J. and M. Robertson MDCCXC.

Christ Dying and Drawing Sinners to Himself or A Survey of our Saviour in His Soul-Suffering, His loveliness in His Death and the Efficacy thereof IN WHICH Some Cases of Soul-trouble in weak Believers, Grounds of Submission under the Absence of CHRIST, with the Flowings and Heightnings of free Grace are opened. Delivered in Sermons on the Gospel according to John Chap. XII. Ver. 27, 28, 29, 30, 31, 32, 33. Where are also interjected some necessary Digressions, for the Times, touching divers Errors of Antinomians; and a short Vindication of the Doctrine of Protestants, from the Arminian pretended universality of Christ's Dying for all and every one of mankind; the moral and feigned way of irresistable Conversion of Sinners; and what Faith is required of all within the visible Church, for the Want thereof, many are condemned. Edinburgh. Printed by T. Lumisden and J. Robertson for James Weir Merchant in Cesford. MDCCXXVII.

146   Samuel Rutherford

Disputatio Scholastica De Divina Providentia. Variis Praelectionibus, quod attinet ad Summa rerum capita, tradita S. Theologiae Adolescentibus Candidatis in Inclyta Academia Andreapolitana in qua adverfus Jefuitas, Arminianos, Socinianos de Dominio DEI, actione ipfius operosa circa peccatum, concurfu primae caufae, praedeterminatione et contenditur et decertatur. Adjectae funt Difquifitiones Metphyficae de Ente, Poffibli, Dominio Dei in entia et non entia, et variae Quaestiones quae ad uberiorem et exquisitiorem cognitionem Doctrinae de Providentia Divina imprimis conducunt. Studiis et induftria Samuelis Retorfortis S. Theologicae Profefforis in celebri et Inclyta Academia Andreapolitana. Edinburgh. Excudebant Haeredes Georgii Anderfoni, pro Roberto Brouno, funtque venales in latere plateae Boreali, haud multum supra crucem ad infigne Solis Anno. DOM M. DC. L.

Examen Arminianismi Conscriptum and difcipulis dictum a Doctifsimo Clarifsimoque Viro D. SAMUELE RHETORFORTE SS. Theol. in Academia Scotiae Sanctandreana Doctore and Profeffore Recenfitum and editum MATTHIA NETHENO SS. Th. D. and Profefs ULTRAJECTI Ex. Officina ANTONII SMYTEGELT, Bibliopolae Anno 1668.

Exercitationes Apologeticae Pro Divina Gratia In quibus vindicatur doctrina orthodoxa de divinis decretis, et Dei tum aeterni decreti tum gratiae efficacis operationis, cum hominis libertate confociatione et fubordinatione amica. Adversus Iacobum Arminium ejufque affeclas, et Iefuitas imprimis vero Fran. Suarezium, Gabri. Vofquezium, Lodiv. Molinam, Leonard, Leffium, Pet. Fonfecum et Robertum Bellarminium. Studio et Industria. SAMUELIS RHAETORFORTIUS. Ecclefiae Anwetorifis in Gallovidia Scotiae Provincia Paftoris. Imperifis Johnannis Dhuringe, Bibliopolae, Anno, 1651.

Influences of the Life of Grace or A Practical Treatise concerning The way, manner and means of having and improving of Spiritual Difpositions, and quickning influences from Christ the Refurrection and the Life. London, Printed for T.C. for Andrew Crook, and are to be sold by James Davies at the gilded Acorn near the little North door in St Paul's Church-yard, 1659.

Lex Rex, The Law and the Prince A dispute for the just Prerogative of King and People Containing the Reasons and caufes of the most neceffary Defensive Wars of the Kingdom of Scotland, and of their expedition for the ayd and help of their dear Brethren of England In which their Innocency is asserted and a full Answer is given to a Seditious Pamphlet, intituled Sacro-fancta Regum Majesftas or The Sacred and Royall Prerogative of Chriftian Kings Under the Name of J.A. But penned by Jo: Maxwell the Excommunicate P. Prelate With a Scripturall Confutation of the ruinous grounds of W. Barclay, H. Grotius, H. Arnifaeus, Ant de Domi. P. Bishop of Spalato and of other late Anti-Magiftratical Royalifts; as the author of Offorianium, D. Fern, E. Symmons, the Doctors of Aberdeen In XLIV Questions. Published by Authority. London: Printed for John Field, and are to be sold at his shop upon Addle-Hill, near Baynards-Castle. Octob. 7. 1644.

The Covenant of Life Opened, or, A Treatise of the Covenant of Grace containing something of The Nature of the Covenant of Works, The Sovereignty of God, The extent of the death of Christ, The nature and properties of the Covenant of Grace and efpecially of The Covenant of Suretyship or Redemption between the Lord, and the Son Jesus Christ, Infant rights to Jesus Christ, the Seal of Baptisme, With some Practicall Questions and Observations. Edinburgh. Printed by Andro Anderson for Robert Broun and are to be sold at his Shop at the Sign of the Sun. Anno 1655.

The Divine Right of Church Government and Excommunication or A peaceable dispute for the perfection of the holy Scripture in point of Ceremonies and Church Government: in which The removal of the Service Book is justified. The six Books of Tho: Erastus against Excommunication are briefly examin'd; with a Vindication of that eminent Divine Theod: Beza against the Aspersions of Erastus: The Arguments of Mr. William Pryn, Rich: Hooker, Dr. Morton, Dr. Jackson, Dr. John Forbes, and the Doctors of Aberdeen: Touching Will-worship, Ceremonies, Imagery, Idolatry, Things Indifferent, An Ambulatory Government; The due and just Power of the Magistrate in matters of Religion, and the Arguments of Mr Pryn, in so far as they side with Erastus, and modestly discussed To which is added, A brief Tractate of Scandal; with an Answer to the new Doctrine of the

Doctors of Aberdeen, touching Scandal. Published by Authority.
London: Printed by John Field for Christopher Meredith at the Crane
in Paul's Church-yard. MDCXLVI.

*The Due Right of Presbyteries or A Peaceable Plea for the
Government of the Church of Scotland* Wherein is examined (1) The
way of the Church of Christ in New England, in Brotherly equality,
and independency, or co-ordination, without subjection of one Church
to another. (2) Their apology for the said Government, their answers
to thirty and two questions are considered. (3) A Treatise for a Church
Covenant is discussed. (4) The Arguments of Mr Robinson in his
justification of separation are discovered. (5) His Treatise, called,
The peoples Plea for the exercise of prophecy, is tryed. (6) Diverse
late arguments against presbyteriall government, and the power of
synods are discussed, the power of the Prince in matters ecclesiastical
modestly considered, and divers incident controversies resolved.
London. Printed by E. Griffin, for Richard Whittaker and Andrew
Crook and are to be sold at their Shops in St. Paul's Church-yard
1644.

*The Last and Heavenly Speeches and Glorious Departure of John,
Viscount Kenmure.* Edinburgh. Printed by Evan Tyler, Printer to the
King's most Excellent Majesty, 1649.

Further editions:
*The Last Speech and Dying Words of the Right Honourable John,
Viscount of Kenmure in Galloway,* who departed this life September
12th, 1634: Printed by William Gray and sold at his house at Magdalen
Chapel within the Cowgate, Edinburgh, 1749, (Prefaced by Thomas
Clark, Edinburgh, January I, 1749).

*The Last and Heavenly Speeches? and Glorious Departure of John,
Viscount Kenmure* within an Introductory Memoir and Notes by
Thomas Murray, Author of *The Literary History of Galloway,*
London, 1827.

*The Protestation of diverse Ministers Against The Proceedings of
the late Commission of the Church of Scotland as Also Against the
lawfulnesse of the prefesnt pretended Assembly.* Printed at Leith by
Evan Tyler. Anno. Dom. 1651.

GENERAL BIBLIOGRAPHY (Works quoted and consulted).

Primary sources

Baillie, R. *Letters and Journals*, 3 Vols., Alex. Laurie, Edinburgh, 1841.

Balfour, J. *Annals*, 3 Vols., W. Aitchison, Edinburgh, 1824.

Carruthers, S.W.(ed). *Everyday Work of the Westminster Assembly*, Presbyterian Soc. of America and Pres. Hist. Soc. of England, Philadelphia, 1943.

Donne, J. *Sermons*, Nonesuch Press, 1967.

Dickinson, C., Donaldson, G. and Milne, I. (eds). *A Source Book of Scottish History*, 2 Vols. Nelson and Sons, Edinburgh and New York, 1958.

Edinburgh Town Council Records, 1636 and 1638.

Gillespie, G.*Assembly of Divines,* February, 1644–January, 1645. Ogle, Oliver and Boyd, Edinburgh, 1846.

Guthrie, J. *Memoirs*, Oliphant, Edinburgh, 1748.

Hobbes, T.*Leviathan,* (ed. Lindsay, A.D.), Dent and Sons, London, 1928.

James, I. *Basilikon Doron*, (ed. Craigie, J.), Blackwood, London, 1944.

James, I. *Political Works*, (ed. McIlwain, C.H.), Harvard Univ. Press, Cambridge, Mass., 1918.

Lightfoot, R. *Letters*, (ed. J.R. Pitman), Dove, London, 1824.

Livingstone, J. *Autobiography,* Duncan, Glasgow, 1754.

Melville, J.*Autobiography and Diary*, (ed. Pitcairn, R.) Wodrow Soc. Edinburgh, 1842.

Mitchell, G.A.F. and Christie, C. (eds). *Records of the Commissioners of the General Assemblies of the C. of S.,* 1646-1652, Edin. Univ. Press, Edinburgh, 1907.

Mitchell, G.A.F. & Struthers, J. *Minutes of the Westminster Assembly*, Blackwood, London, 1874.

Patrick, D. (ed.). *Statuta Ecclesiae,* Edin. Univ. Press, Edinburgh, 1907.

Peterkin, A. (ed.).*Records of the Church of Scotland*, 1638-1649, John Sutherland, Edinburgh, 1838.

Peterkin, A. (ed). *The Booke of the Universall Kirk of Scotland*, Edinburgh, Printing and Publishing Coy., Edinburgh, 1839.

Pitman, J.R. (ed). *Journal of the Westminster Assembly,* Jan 1, 1643-Decr. 31, 1644, Dove, London, 1824.

Records of the Commission of the Assembly of the Church of Scotland, Scottish History Society Edinburgh, 1892.

St. Andrews and Cupar Presbytery Records, 1637.

Scottish Historical Society, (ed.). *Consultations of the Ministers of Edinburgh*, 1632-1660, Edin. Univ. Press. Edinburgh.

Thomas, E. *Gangraena*, (3rd. ed.), London, 1646.

Warriston, A. *Diary*, 1632-1639 (ed. Johnston, A.), Edin. Univ. Press, Edinburgh, 1911.

Wodrow, R. *Analecta*, (ed. J. Sashman), Edin. Univ. Printing Club, Edinburgh, 1842.

Biographical

Black, G. *Surnames of Scotland*, New York Public Library, New York, 1965.

Gilmour, R. *Samuel Rutherford*, Oliphant, Anderson and Ferrier, Edin. 1904.

Hanna, W. *Memoirs of Dr. Chalmers,* Sutherland & Knox, Edinburgh, 1851.

Innes, T. *Samuel Rutherford*, Studies in Scottish History, London, 1892.

Lee, S. (ed.). *Dictionary of National Biography*, Smith-Elder, London, 1897.

McCrie, T. *Life of Andrew Melville*, Blackwood, Edinburgh, 1827.

Meek, D.(ed.). *George Gillespie*, Ogle, Oliver and Boyd, Edinburgh, 1846.

Murray T. *Life of Rutherford*, W. Oliphant, Edinburgh, 1827.

Pedigree of Rutherford, Edgeston, Hunthill and Hundalee, (in the possession of the Rutherford Family, Rutherford Lodge, Rutherford).

Reid, J. *Memoirs of the Lives and Writings of those Eminent Divines*, who convened the famous Assembly at Westminster, Stephen and Andrew Young, Paisley, 1815.

Row, W. *Life of Blair* (ed. McCrie, T.), Blackwood, Edinburgh, 1848.

Rutherford, J. *Rutherford of that Ilk*, Scott and Ferguson, Edinburgh, 1884.

Thomson, A. *Samuel Rutherford* (4th Edition), Hodder and Stoughton, London, 1889.

Whyte, A. *Samuel Rutherford and some of his Correspondents*, Oliphant, Anderson and Ferrier, Edinburgh, 1894.

Wylie, J.A. *Scottish Worthies*, Mackenzie, London, (undated).

Ecclesiastical History

Alexander, H.G. *Religion in England*, 1558-1602, Univ. of London Press, London, 1968.

Burleigh, J.H.S. *A Church History of Scotland*, O.U.P., London, 1960.

Calderwood, D. *History of the Kirk of Scotland*, Wodrow Society, Edinburgh, 1849.

Donaldson, G. *Church and Nation through Sixteen Centuries*, S.C.M., London, 1960.

Donaldson, G. *The Scottish Reformation*, C.U.P., Cambridge, 1960.

Fisher, H.A.L. *History of the Church*, Hodder & Stoughton, London.

Henderson, G.D. *The Claims of the Church of Scotland*, Hodder & Stoughton, London, 1951.

Hetherington, W.M. *History of the Westminster Assembly of Divines*, Gemmel, Edinburgh, 1878.

Mitchell, G.A.F. *The Westminster Assembly, Its History and Standards,* Nisbet, London, 1883.

Moffatt, J. *The Presbyterian Churches*, Methuen, London, 1928.

Ogilvie, J.D. *Resolutioner-Protester Controversy, Transactions of the Edinburgh Bibliographical Society*, Vol. XIV, 1930.

Ross, J. *History of Congregational Independency in Scotland*, MacLehose, Glasgow, 1900.

Taylor, M.C. *Historical Account of the Union between Church and State*, (St. Giles Lectures), McNiven and Wallace, Edinburgh, 1886.

Social and Political History

Bower, A. *History of Edinburgh University*, Oliphant, Waugh and Innes, Edinburgh, 1817.

Crawford, T. *History of Edinburgh University*, McNeill, Edinburgh, 1808.

Dalzel, A. *History of Edinburgh University*, Edmaston and Douglas, Edinburgh, 1862.

Davies, G. *Early Stuarts*, Clarendon Press, Oxford, 1936.

Dickinson, C. *Scotland from the Earliest Times to 1603*, Nelson, Edinburgh, 1961.

Firth, C.H.(ed.). *Scotland and the Protectorate*, Univ. of Edin. Press, Edinburgh, 1899.

Firth, C.H.(ed.). *Scotland under the Commonwealth*, Univ. of Edin. Press, Edinburgh, 1895.

Gardiner, S.R. (ed). *Charles II and Scotland*, 1650, Scottish Hist. Society, Edinburgh, 1894.

Major, J. *History of Greater Britain*, Scottish History Society, Edinburgh, 1892.

Smout, T.C. *A History of the Scottish People*, 1560-1830, Collins, Glasgow, 1973.

Other Works

Bush, D. *English Literature in the Earlier Seventeenth Century*, (2nd Ed.) O.U.P. Oxford, 1962.

Chambers, W. and R. *Encyclopaedia of English Literature*, 3 Vols. London and Edinburgh, 1903.

Jones, R. *Studies in Mystical Religion*, Macmillan, London, 1909.

Leuba, J. M. *Psychology of Religious Mysticism*, Kegan-Paul, London, 1925.

McLeod, J. *Scottish Theology*, Edinburgh, 1943.

REFERENCES

Chapter 1

1. Gilmour, R., *Samuel Rutherford*, Oliphant, Anderson and Ferrier, Edinburgh, 1904, p. 11 (hereafter referred to as Gilmour).

2. Burleigh, J.H.S.,*A Church History of Scotland*, O.U.P, London, 1960, p. 153 (hereafter, Burleigh).

3. Smout, T.C., *A History of the Scottish People*, 1560-1830, Collins, Glasgow, 1973, p. 57 (hereafter, Smout).

4. *Statuta Ecclesiae*, Edinburgh University Press, (for the Scottish History Society), Introduction by D. Patrick, 1907, Preface.

5. Henderson, G.D., *The Claims of the Church of Scotland*, Hodder and Stoughton, London, 1951, p. 81.

6. Smout, p. 59.

7. Burleigh, p. 156.

8. Moffatt, J., *The Presbyterian Churches,* Methuen, London, 1928, p. 48.

9. Donaldson, G., *Church and Nation through Sixteen Centuries*, S.C.M., London, 1960, p. 63.

10. Ross, J., *A History of Congregational Independency in Scotland*, MacLehose, Glasgow, 1900, p. 3.

11. *ibid.* p. 6.

12. *Dictionary of National Biography*, ed. S. Lee, Smith Elder, London, 1897, Vol. xxi, p. 324.

13. Taylor, M.C., *Historical Account of the Union between Church and State*; *England and Scotland*, (St. Giles Lectures), Lecture 1 in *Church and People,* McNiven and Wallace, Edinburgh, 1886.

14. *The Booke of the Universall Kirk of Scotland*, ed. A. Peterkin, (for Wodrow Soc.), Edinburgh Printing and Publishing Co., Edinburgh, 1839, p. 151 (hereafter *B.U.K.S.*).

15. *ibid.* p.152.

16. *ibid.* p. 175.

17. *ibid.* p. 178.

18. Melville, J., *Autobiography and Diary, 1556-1610*, ed. R. Pitcairn, Wodrow Soc., Edinburgh, 1842, p. 370.

19. *B.U.K.S.* p. 530.

20. *ibid.*

21. James, I., *Basilikon Doron*, from *A Source Book of Scottish History*, ed. C. Dickinson, Nelson and Sons, London, 1954, vol. 3, pp. 50ff.

22. *B.U.K.S.*, p. 444

23. Smout, p. 60.

24. Dickinson, C., *Scotland from the Earliest Times to 1603*, Nelson, Edinburgh, 1961, p. 354.

25. *Letters of Samuel Rutherford*, ed. A.A. Bonar (1863 edition), vol. 1, p.2, (hereafter, Letters).

26. *ibid.* vol. 1, p. 390, footnote.

27. *ibid.* From St. Andrews, June 15, 1655, vol. 2, p. 390. By this date it appears that Nisbet was annexed to Craigling. The recipient of this letter, John Scott, is designated by Bonar, 'minister of Oxam', Oxam being only two miles from Nisbet.

28. Murray, T., *Life of Rutherford*, W. Oliphant, Edinburgh, 1827, p. 2 (hereafter, Murray).

29. *Records of the General Assembly Commission*, (Scot. Hist. Soc.), Edinburgh, vol. 58, p. 17.

30. *Pedigree of Rutherford, Edgeston, Hunthill and Hundalee,* in the possession of the Rutherford family, Rutherford Lodge, Rutherford (hereafter, Pedigree). The name 'Rutherford' excites interest. A perusal of the pedigree of Rutherford reveals a variation of spelling over the centuries as we might expect. In the charter granted by David I it is spelt Rodyforde, by 1215 'i' had replaced the 'y', while in Edward I's reign, it was Rothiforde, and in the fifteenth century a 'u' replaced both the 'o's', to read Ruthifurde. In the seventeenth century the final 'e' was dropped.

31. Rutherford, Sir John, *Rutherford of the Ilk*, Scott and Ferguson, Edinburgh, 1884. p. xiii.

32. *vide.* Bibliography, Writings of Rutherford.

33. Black, G., *Surnames of Scotland*, New York Public Library, New York, 1965, p. 704.

34. Thomson, A., *Samuel Rutherford*, (4th Edition), Hodder and Stoughton, London, 1889, p. 11. (Hereafter Thomson).

35. *Letters*, vol. 1, p. 2.

36. Gilmour, pp. 24-5.

37. The College in Rutherford's day had been but lately founded in 1582. Its first Principal was the renowned theologian Robert Rollock who held the post until 1599. When Rutherford enrolled, the Principal was one called Boyd, a staunch Presbyterian, dismissed for this reason by James VI. He was a man who greatly influenced Rutherford. There can be no doubt that Rutherford imbibed from him not only his adherence to Presbyterian government, but also his supralapsarian theology. Boyd had spent some fifteen years teaching in France, where he became thoroughly conversant with Huguenot theology.

38. Dalzel, A., *History of Edinburgh University,* Edmaston and Douglas, Edinburgh, 1862, vol. 2, p. 79 (hereafter Dalzel).

39. Thomson, p. 13.

40. Gilmour, p. 39.

41. *Letters*, pp. 3-4.

42. *ibid.* p. 11.

43. Dalzel, vol. 2, p. 84.

44. *ibid.* vol. 2, pp. 106-7. Also the Town Council Record for 24:8:1638. This record shows that both were dismissed from their Chairs on 5:9:1638.

45. *ibid.* p. 84.

46. Record for 3:2:1626.

47. Dalzel. vol. 2, p. 84.

48. *ibid.* vol. 2, p. 85.

49. *Letters.* From Aberdeen, March 9, 1637, vol. 1, p. 285. William Rigg, a Baillie of Edinburgh, was a staunch opponent of the introduction of prelacy. In March, 1624, a Committee of the Privy Council, by the authority of the King, deprived him of his office, fined him £50,000 (Scot.) and imprisoned him in Blackness Castle until the fine was paid, and thereafter in Orkney, a sentence which was later mitigated. He died January 2nd, 1644.

50. *ibid.* From Aberdeen, March 14th, 1637, vol. 1, p. 354. The recipient of this letter cannot be identified. Bonar points out in his foreword to the letter that the name was common, and states she may have been one of his Anwoth parishioners.

51. *ibid.* From Aberdeen, June 16th, 1637, vol. 1, p. 436. Earlston theYounger was William Gordon, a country Laird, whom John Howie described as 'a gentleman of good parts and endowments, a man devoted to religion and godliness' (Whyte, A., *Samuel Rutherford and Some of His Correspondents*, Oliphant, Anderson and Ferrier, Edinburgh and London, 1894, pp. 96-7 [hereafter, S.R.C.].) He died after being shot by English dragoons, while on his way to join the Covenanters at Bothwell Bridge.

52. *ibid.* To Robert Stuart, from Aberdeen, June 17th, 1637, vol. 1, p. 455. Robert Stuart was probably the son of Ayr's Provost.

Chapter Two

1. Gilmour, p. 34.

2. *Letters*, vol. 1, p. 4.

3. Thomson, p. 20.

4. Hanna, W., *Memoirs of Dr. Chalmers*, Sutherland and Knox, Edinburgh, 1851, vol. 3, p. 130.

5. Thomson, p. 21.

6. Thomson, p. 22.

7. Gilmour, p. 38.

8. *Letters*, Preface to letter addressed to William Dalgleish, minister of Anwoth, Kirkdale and Kirkmabreck joint charges, vol. 1, p. 291.

9. *ibid.* From Anwoth, July 27th, 1628, vol. 1, p. 43. Viscountess Kenmure was Lady Jane Campbell, one of the Campbells of Argyll. Her marriage to the dissolute John Gordon, Viscount Kenmure, was not a happy

one. From the 47 letters Rutherford penned to her, we gather that he was a source of strength to her in her trials.

10. *ibid.* From Anwoth, 1633 (undated), vol. 1, p. 107.

11. *ibid.* From Anwoth (undated), vol. 1, p. 138. Marion McNaught to whom Rutherford wrote some 45 letters, was the wife of William Fullarton, the Provost of Kirkcudbright, and the niece of Lord Kenmure, S.R.C. pp. 19-28 (hereafter M.M.).

12. Wodrow, R., *Analecta*, ed. J. Sashman, Edin. Univ. Printing Club, Edinburgh, 1842, vol. 4, p. 53 (hereafter Wodrow).

13. Wylie, J.A., *Scottish Worthies*, Mackenzie, London (undated), p. 209, also *Letters*, vol. 1, p. 4.

14. Murray, p. 37.

15. *Letters.* From Anwoth, July 8, 1635, vol. 1, p. 148.

16. *ibid.* From Aberdeen to John Henderson, March 14, 1637, vol. 1, p.350.

17. *ibid.* From Anwoth, July 8, 1635, vol. 1, p. 148.

18. Gilmour, p. 54.

19. *op. cit.* p. 24.

20. *vide* Bibliography, Sermons.

21. Bonar, A.A., *Quaint Sermons of Samuel Rutherford*, Hodder & Stoughton, London, 1885, pp. 136ff. (hereafter, Q.S.).

22. *ibid.* p. 103.

23. *ibid.* p. 125.

24. *ibid.* p. 125.

25. *ibid.* p. 125.

26. *ibid.* p. 111.

27. *ibid.* p. 117.

28. *ibid.* p. 119.

29. *ibid.* p. 122.

30. *Tryal and Truimph of Faith*, London, 1645, Preface.

31. *Q.S.,* p. 218.

32. *ibid.* p. 279.

33. *ibid.* p. 225.

34. *ibid.* p. 205.

35. *ibid.* p. 206.

36. *ibid.* p. 277.

37. An exposition of Essay. 8.17. London, 1645.

38. *ibid.*

39. *Q.S.* p. 221.

40. *ibid.* p. 218.

41. *ibid.* p. 221.

42. *ibid.* p. 222.

43. *ibid.* p. 86.

44. *ibid.* p. 97.

45. Bonar, A.A., *Twelve Communion Sermons,* Chas. Goss and Co., Glasgow, 1876, p. 234.

46. Bush, D., *English Literature in the Earlier Seventeenth Century,* (2nd Ed.) O.U.P. Oxford, 1962, p. 319.

47. Donne, J., *Complete Verse and Selected Prose*, ed. J. Hayward, Nonesuch Press, London, 1972, p. 558.

48. Letters. To Alex. Colville, June 23, 1637, vol. 2, p. 48. Alex. Colville of Blair in Fife was one of the judges disposed towards Rutherford, when brought before the High Commission in 1630. He was a church elder and delegate to the General Assemblies of 1645, '46 and '48.

49. *ibid.* From Aberdeen to parishioners, July 13, 1637, vol. 2, p. 87.

50. *ibid.* From Aberdeen, Sept. 23, 1637, vol. 2, p. 193.

51. Wodrow, vol. 1, p. 205.

52. Gilmour, p. 41.

53. Thomson, p. 23.

54. *ibid.* pp. 26-27.

55. *ibid.* p. 26.

56. Gilmour, p. 39.

57. *Letters*. From Anwoth, 1634, vol. 1, p. 153.

58. *ibid.* To Alex. Gordon of Earlston, September 5, 1636, vol. 1, p. 172. Alex. Gordon was the great grandson of Alex. Gordon, nicknamed 'Strong Sandy', because of his Samson-like strength. He was the leader of the Presbyterian cause in Galloway. He was banished from his native county for resisting the Bishop of Glasgow. He was a member of the General Assembly of 1638, and M.P. for Galloway in 1641. He refused a knighthood when offered it by the Crown. *S.R.C.* pp. 86-94.

59. *ibid.* To Robert Gordon of Knockbreck, September 5, 1636, vol. 1, p. 173. Robert Gordon was Laird of Knockbreck, a close friend of Rutherford, whom Livingstone records was much employed in Parliaments and public meetings after 1638. *S.R.C.* p. 104.

60. *ibid.* January 24, 1637, vol. 1, p. 222. Lord Craighall was the son of the eminent lawyer, Sir Thomas Hope. He became a Privy Councillor and his name appears as a member of the General Assemblies, 1645-49.

61. *ibid.* 1637, vol. 1, p. 246.

62. *ibid.* To James Bruce, March 14, 1637, vol. 1, p. 344. James Bruce was minister of Kingsbarn, Fife.

63. *ibid.* March 11, 1637, vol. 1, p. 309.

64. *ibid.* From Anwoth to M.M., June 6, 1627, vol. 1, p. 35. (Wrongly dated as 1624 in editions prior to 1863.)

65. *ibid.* From Aberdeen, March 6, 1637, vol. 1, p. 35. John Gordon of Cardoness, the Elder, was descended from Gordon of Lochinvar. He was the first of 188 signatories who petitioned in 1638 for Rutherford's retention as minister of Anwoth.

66. *ibid.* From Aberdeen, March 6, 1637; vol. 1, p. 263.

67. *ibid.* 1637, vol. 1, p. 389.

68. *ibid.* From Aberdeen, to Margaret Ballantyne, 1637, vol. 1, p. 202. Margaret Ballantyne was probably one of his parishioners.

69. *ibid.* From Anwoth, 1630, vol. 1, p. 37.

70. *ibid.* From Aberdeen, March 14, 1637, vol. 1, p. 346. John Gordon was Laird of Rusco, three miles from Anwoth.

71. 'Discipline and Welfare in the Seventeenth Century Scottish Parish,' *Scottish History Society Records*, vol. XIX, p. 171.

72. *Letters.* From Aberdeen, to the Elder Cardoness, 1637 (undated), vol. 1, p. 389.

73. *ibid.* From Aberdeen, June 16, 1637, vol. 1, p. 433.

74. *ibid.* From Aberdeen, 1637 (undated), vol. 2, p. 26.

75. *ibid.* From Aberdeen, to Earlston the Younger, June 16, 1637, vol. 1, p. 345.

76. *ibid.* From Anwoth, to a lady on the death of her daughter, April 23, 1628, vol. 1, p. 37.

77. *ibid.* From Anwoth, January 15, 1629, vol. 1, pp. 44-45.

78. *ibid.* August 4, 1636, vol. 1, p. 168. Robert Cunningham had previously been chaplain to the Earl of Buccleuch's regiment in Holland. On his return he became minister of Holywood in N. Ireland on November 9, 1615. On August 12, 1636, along with other ministers he was deposed from his charge for refusing to subscribe to certain canons, one of which ordered the posture of kneeling at the Lord's Supper. He moved to Scotland, but died shortly after at Irvine on March 29, 1637.

79. *ibid.* From Anwoth, vol. 1, p. 50.

80. *ibid.* From Anwoth, vol. 1, p. 54.

81. Bonar believed that John Hamilton was a relative of his wife, Euphan Hamilton. *Letters,* footnote, vol. 1, p. 54.

82. *ibid.* To M.M., from Anwoth, 1630 (undated), vol. 1, pp. 54-55.

83. *ibid.* From Anwoth, June 26, 1630, vol. 1 p. 60.

84. *ibid.* From Anwoth, April 29, 1634, vol. 1, p. 114.

85. *ibid.* From Anwoth, June 26, 1630, vol. 1, p. 60.

86. Thomson, p. 41.

87. *Letters.* From Anwoth, September 14, 1629, vol. 1, p. 48.

88. *ibid.* March 14, 1637, vol. 1, p. 346.

89. *ibid.* From Anwoth, to M.M. February 1, 1630, vol. 1, p. 55.

90. *ibid.* From Aberdeen, to Earlston the Younger, 1637 (undated), vol. 2, p. 18.

91. *ibid.* From Anwoth, January 4, 1632, vol. 1, p. 81.

92. *ibid.* From Anwoth, to Lady Kenmure, January 15, 1629, vol. 1, p. 45.

93. *ibid.* From Anwoth, 1634, (undated), vol. 1, p. 136.

94. *ibid.* From Anwoth, to M.M., 1634 (undated), vol. 1, p. 132.

95. *ibid.* From Anwoth to M.M., November 17, 1629, vol. 1, p. 50.

96. *ibid.* From Anwoth, June 2, 1631 (undated), vol. 1, p. 69.

97. *ibid.* From Anwoth, to M.M., 1631 (undated), vol. 1, p. 74.

98. *ibid.* From Anwoth, 1631 (undated), vol. 1, p. 76.

99. *ibid.* From Anwoth, to M.M., May 30, 1634, vol. 1, pp. 116-7.

100. *ibid.* From Anwoth, to M.M., 1633 (wrongly dated in Bonar), vol. 1, p. 141.

101. *ibid.* From Anwoth, June 26, vol. 1, p. 59.

102. *ibid.* From Anwoth, to Lady Kenmure, June 26, 1630, vol. 1, p.59.

103. *ibid.* From Edinburgh, to M.M., December, 1634, vol. 1, p.147.

104. *ibid.* From Anwoth, to M.M., 1635 (undated), vol. 1, p. 147.

105. *ibid.* From Aberdeen, to John Stuart, Provost of Ayr, 1637 (undated), vol. 1, p. 375.

106. *ibid.* From Edinburgh, to M.M., 1637 (undated), vol. 1, p. 375.

107. *ibid.* From Edinburgh, to M.M., 1636 (undated) vol. 1, p. 161.

Chapter 3

1. *Letters.* From Edinburgh, September 15, 1636, vol. 1, p. 173.

2. *ibid.* From Edinburgh, April 5, 1636, vol. 1, p. 155.

3. *ibid.* Sketch, vol. 1, p. 13.

4. *ibid.* From Edinburgh, September 5, 1636, vol. 1, p. 173.

5. *ibid.* From Edinburgh, September 5, 1636, vol. 1, p. 171.

6. *ibid.* To Rob. Gordon, September 20, 1636, vol. 1, p. 174 (*vide* chapter 2, reference 59).

7. *ibid.* To Lady Kenmure, November 22, 1636, vol. 1, p. 179

8. *ibid.* To Lady Boyd (undated), 1637, vol. 1, p. 197. Lady Boyd, the former Christian Hamilton, was the eldest daughter of the first Earl of Haddington. Her first husband was the ninth Lord Lindsay of Byres, who died in 1616. Her second husband was the sixth Lord Boyd, who died in August, 1628. She was an ardent Presbyterian, noted for her personal piety. *S.R.C.* pp. 50-58.

9. *ibid.* November 22, 1636, vol. 1, pp. 179-180.

10. *ibid.* To Alex. Colville of Blair, February 19, 1637, vol. 1, p. 251 (*vide* chapter 2, reference 48).

11. *ibid.* To John Meine, March 14, 1637, vol. 1, p. 352. John Meine, a merchant of Edinburgh, was a supporter of the Presbyterian cause. Because of his support for nonconforming ministers before the Court of High Commission, he was banished to Wigtown by the Privy Council, under the King's orders. The sentence, however, was suspended later. His objection to kneeling at communion occasioned a summons before the Privy Council and banishment to Elgin until the death of James VI on 27th March, 1625. His first wife was Barbara Hamilton, sister of the first wife of Robert Blair.

160

12. *ibid.* To William Gordon, February 20, 1637, vol.1, p. 253 (*vide* chapter 1, reference 51).

13. *ibid.* To John Fleming, November 13, 1636, vol. 1, p. 177. Little is known of John Fleming. He appears to have been a Bailie of Leith and brother of a teacher in Kirkcudbright, who was summoned before the Court of High Commission in November, 1636 and deprived of his post.

14. *ibid.* To Hugh McKail, November 22, 1636, vol. 1, p. 184. Hugh McKail was minister of Irvine. Rutherford would have liked to have seen him succeed Robert Glendinning at Kirkcudbright. Later he moved to Edinburgh, and died in 1660, being buried in Greyfriars churchyard.

15. *ibid.* (undated), 1636, vol. 1, p. 188.

16. *ibid.* To Alex. Gordon, February 16, 1637, vol. 1, p. 248.

17. *ibid.* From Edinburgh, to Alex. Gordon, September 5, 1636, vol. 1, p. 172 (*vide* as above).

18. *ibid.* To William Gordon, February 20, 1637, vol. 1, p. 253 (*vide* chapter 1, reference 51).

19. *ibid.* February 9, 1637, vol. 1, p. 238.

20. *ibid.* (undated), 1637, vol. 1, pp. 244-5.

21. *ibid.* February 16, vol. 2, p. 249.

22. *ibid.* To M.M. March 11, 1637, vol. 1, p. 309.

23. *ibid.* (undated), 1637, vol. 2, p. 21.

24. *ibid.* July 13, 1637, vol. 2, p. 89.

25. *ibid.* To his parishioners, September 23, 1637, vol. 1, p. 198.

26. *ibid.* To Lady Boyd (undated), 1637, vol. 1, p. 198 (*vide*, this chapter reference 8).

27. *ibid.* June 11, 1637, vol. 1, p. 450.

28. *ibid.* March 13, 1637, vol. 1, p. 341.

29. *ibid.* February 7, 1637, vol. 1, p. 231.

30. *ibid.* (undated), 1637, vol. 1, p. 375.

31. *ibid.* To George Gillespie, March 15, 1637, vol. 1, p. 342. George Gillespie was sometime minister in Kirkcaldy. He was licensed to preach prior to 1638, the year in which he was ordained minister of Wemyss. In 1642 he moved as minister to an Edinburgh church, where he continued until his death in 1648, at the early age of 36. He was a Commissioner to the Westminster Assembly in 1643.

32. *ibid.* (undated), 1637, vol. 1, p. 375.

33. *ibid.* (undated), 1637, vol. 1, p. 356.

34. *ibid.* To John Stuart, Provost of Ayr (undated), 1637, vol. 1, p. 382.

35. Baillie, R., *Letters and Journals*, Alex. Laurie, Edinburgh, 1841, vol. 1, p.9.

36. *Letters.* February 13, 1637, vol. 1, p. 242.

37. *ibid.* (undated), 1637, vol. 1, p. 452.

38. *ibid.* September 7, 1637, vol. 2, p. 140.

39. *ibid.*

40. Gilmour, p. 191.

41. Davies, G., *The Early Stuarts,* U.U.P. p. 85.

42. *Letters.* To M.M., June, 15, 1637, vol. 1, p. 418.

43. *ibid.* To a Gentlewoman, March 7, 1637, vol. 1, p. 266 (identity of correspondent unknown).

44. *ibid.* To William Livingstone, March 13, 1637, vol. 1, p. 337. William Livingstone was probably one of Rutherford's parishioners.

45. *ibid.* September 21, 1636, vol. 1, p. 175.

46. *ibid.* To Lady Culross, December 30, 1636, vol. 1, p. 190. Lady Culross was Elizabeth Melville, a Lady of the Covenant. Alexander Whyte wrote 'Lady Culross' name will always be held in the tender honour in the innermost circles of our best Scottish Christians, for the hand she had in that wonderful outpouring of God's grace at the Kirk of Shotts on that Thanksgiving Monday in 1636. Under God, the Covenanters' Pentecost was more due to Lady Culross than any other human being – What a mother of Israel was Lady Culross with five hundred children born of her travail in one day' (*S.R.C.* pp. 43-49).

47. *ibid.* To Robert Gordon of Knockbreck, January 1, 1637, vol. 1, p. 195 (*vide* chapter 2, reference 59).

48. *ibid.* March 7, 1637, vol. 1, p. 280.

49. *ibid.* To John Nevay, June 11, 1637, vol. 1, p. 426. John Nevay was minister of New Milns, and chaplain to the Earl of Loudon. A strict Presbyterian, he was ordered out of the country in 1662, on pain of death. He spent the rest of his years in Rotterdam. He had a gift for poetry and was commissioned by the 1647 Assembly to revise 30 of Rous' metrical psalms.

50. *ibid.* To John Fleming, November 13, 1636, vol. 1, p. 177. Nothing is known of Fleming, he may have been an Edinburgh merchant.

51. *ibid.*

52. *ibid.* To Lady Culross, December 1636, vol. 1, p. 190 (*vide* above reference 46).

53. *ibid.* To Lady Kenmure (undated), 1636, vol. 1, p. 182 (*vide* chapter 2, reference 9).

54. *ibid.* To William Rigg of Arthernie, Fife, March 9, 1637, vol. 1, p. 285 (*vide* chapter 1, reference 49).

55. *ibid.* To John Lennox, (undated), 1637, vol. 2, p. 24. John Lennox was Laird of Cally, in the Stewartry of Kirkcudbright. Little is known of him.

56. *ibid.* To Bethsaida Aird, March 14, 1637, vol. 1, p. 354. Although the name Aird was familiar in church circles, nothing is known of this lady. Bonar thinks she may have been a parishioner of Anwoth.

57. *ibid.*

58. *ibid.* To Alex. Gordon of Earlston, February 16, vol. 1, 247 (*vide*

chapter 2, reference 58).

59. *ibid.* To Lady Cardoness, February 20, 1637, vol. 1, p. 255. Lady Cardoness was the wife of John Gordon. *S.R.C.* pp. 35-42.

60. *ibid.* March 7, 1637, vol. 1, p. 276. David Dickson, born 1583, was the only son of a Glasgow merchant. For eight years he was Prof. of Philosophy at Glasgow University. In 1618 he became minister of Irvine. After being summoned before the Court of High Commission he was deprived of his charge and sent to Turriff in Aberdeenshire. He was allowed to return to Irvine in 1623. In 1642 he was appointed Professor of Divinity at Glasgow University and later translated to the same office in Edinburgh. In the Resolutioner-Protester controversy, he took the side of the former.

61. *ibid.* March 7, 1637. vol. 1, p. 283. Robert Douglas may well have been an illegitimate grandson of Queen Mary. For a time he was chaplain in the army of Gustavus Adolphus, King of Sweden, and a great favourite of the sovereign. On returning to Scotland in 1630, he became colleague to the minister of Kirkcaldy. In 1641 he moved to Edinburgh. In 1669, he became minister of Pencaitland, where he died in 1674 and was buried in Edinburgh.

62. To John Nevay, July 1, 1637, vol. 2, p. 50 (*vide* this chapter reference 49).

Chapter 4

1. Reid, J. *Memoirs of the Lives and Writings of the Eminent Divines who convened in the Famous Assembly at Westminster,* Stephen and Andrew Young, Paisley, 1815, p. 549 (hereafter, Memoirs).

2. Hetherington, W.M. *History of the Westminster Assembly of Divines,* Gemmel, Edinburgh, 1878, p. 406 (hereafter, Hetherington).

3. *Memoirs.* p. 350.

4. Peterkin, A. (ed.). *Records of the Church of Scotland, 1638-1649,* John Sutherland, Edinburgh, 1838, p. 109 (hereafter, Peterkin).

5. Baillie, R. *Letters and Journals*, Alex. Laurie, Edinburgh, 1841, vol. 1, p. 99 (hereafter, Baillie).

6. *ibid.* vol. 1. p. 173.

7. *Letters.* From Kirkcudbright, October 1. 1639, vol. 2. p. 250.

8. *ibid.* From St. Andrews, November 22, 1639. vol. 2. p. 261.

9. *ibid.* To Henry Stuart, from St. Andrews, vol. 2. p. 265. Henry Stuart was a Scot, resident in Ireland, who along with his family and a domestic servant, James Gray, refused to swear to the 'Black Oath'. They were taken to Dublin by the Sergeant at arms and subjected to close confinement. On August 10, 1639 they were brought to trial before the Star Chamber. Stuart protested that they had no objection to swearing civil allegiance, but he could not concede unlimited ecclesiastical obedience to the king. Wentworth pronounced sentence upon the defendants and considerable fines were imposed upon each of them, they being detained in Dublin until paid. They

were set free in 1641 (after 1¼ years' imprisonment), but to poverty, Stuart's property having been confiscated by Wentworth. He returned to Scotland in Sept. 1641.

10. Hetherington, p. 119.

11. *Letters*. To Lady Kenmure, from Anwoth, July 27, 1628, vol. 1 p. 42, *vide* also, from Anwoth, February 1. 1630, pp. 53-54 (*vide* chapter 2. reference 9).

12. *ibid.* To Lady Kenmure, January 23, 1643, vol. 1. p. 109.

13. *ibid.* From Anwoth, March 2, vol. 1. p. 110.

14. *ibid.* To M.M. from Anwoth, vol. 1. p. 50.

15. *ibid.* To M.M. from Anwoth, June 2, 1631, vol. 1. p. 69.

16. *ibid.*

17. *ibid.* From Anwoth, 1631 (undated), vol. 1. p. 74.

18. *ibid.* From Anwoth, February 1. 1632, vol. 1 pp. 89-90. John Kennedy was the son of Hugh, Provost of Ayr. He was a member of the Scottish Parliament in 1644-5- 6, for the burgh of Ayr. He was also a member of the General Assemblies of 1642-3-4-6-7.

19. *ibid.* From Anwoth, February 13, 1632, vol. 1. p. 32.

20. *ibid.* From Anwoth, January 14, 1632, vol. 1. p. 86.

21. Arminians were those who accepted the teaching of Arminius or James Harmensen, a Dutch theologian, who maintained the doctrine of free will against Calvin. They came to the fore in England at the end of the sixteenth century. They were also attracted by aspects of Catholic revival, and were ready to adopt the traditions of the pre-reformation church. They became increasingly influential during the reigns of James I and Charles I.

22. *Letters*. To M.M. from Anwoth, (undated), 1631, vol. 1. p. 74.

23. *ibid.* From Aberdeen, (undated), 1637, vol. 1. p. 373.

24. *ibid.* To Lady Boyd, from St. Andrews, (undated), 1640, vol. 2. p. 304. (vide chapter 3 reference 7).

25. *ibid.* From Aberdeen, July 31, 137, vol. 2. p. 89; also from Aberdeen, September 23, 1637, vol. 2. pp. 193-94.

26. Romans 1:25.

27. *Letters*. To Ephraim Melvin, from Aberdeen (undated), 1637, vol. 1. p. 237. Ephraim Melvin was the first ordained minister of Queensferry and later of Linlithgow, where he died.

28. *ibid.* To Lord Craighall, from Aberdeen, June 8, 1637, vol. 1. p. 408 (*vide* chapter 2. reference 60).

29. *ibid.* From Aberdeen, September 23, 1637, vol . 2. p. 194.

30. *ibid.* To M.M. from Aberdeen, 1637 (not 1633 as dated by Bonar), vol. 2. p. 242.

31. *ibid.* To his parishioners, from Aberdeen, July 13, 1637, vol. 2. p. 89.

32. *ibid.*

33. *ibid.* To John Fergushill, minister of Ochiltree, 1637 (undated), vol. 1. pp. 463-64.

34. *ibid.* To John Stuart, Provost of Ayr, (undated), 1637, vol. 1. p. 374. John Stuart was a man of property, a benefactor to those in distress, who later found himself in such a condition. He intended to emigrate to New England, but was prevented by bad weather.

35. Baillie, vol. 2. p. 481.

36. *ibid.* vol. 2. p. 159.

37. Mitchell, G.A.F. and Christie, C. (Eds), *Records of the Commissioners of the General Assemblies of the Church of Scotland 1646-1652*, Edin. Univ. Press, Edinburgh, 1907. (26.11.46) vol. 2. p. 49 (hereafter, Records).

38. *ibid.* 11. 11. 46). vol. 2. p. 49.

39. *ibid.* 15. 1. 47). vol. 2. p. 189.

40. *ibid.* 13. 1. 47). vol. 2. p. 187.

41. Carruthers, S.W. (ed.). *Everyday Work of the Westminister Assembly*, Presbyterian Soc. in America and Presbyterian Hist. Soc. of England, Philadelphia, 1943, p. 26. (hereafter, Carruthers).

42. Hetherington, p. 130.

43. Baillie, vol. 2. p. 110.

44. Hetherington, p. 134 ff..

45. *ibid.* p. 140.

46. *ibid.* p. 141.

47. Carruthers, p. 75.

48. Session 76, Oct. 17, 1643.

49. Gillespie, G. *Assembly of Divines, Feb. 1644–Jan. 1645* (ed. D. Meek), from unpublished MSS, Ogle, Oliver and Boyd, Edinburgh, 1846, p. 3.

50. vol. 2. p. 110.

51. Session 89. November 6.

52. *A Peaceable Plea for Paul's Presbyterie in Scotland*, Bartlet, London, 1642, p. 314. (*vide*, Bibliography of Rutherford's Writings.)

53. *Letters*. To Lady Kenmure, from London, March 4, 1644, vol. 2 p. 131 (*vide*, chapter 2. reference 9).

54. *Records*. 1 - 1 - 47, vol. 2, p. 184.

55. *Letters*. To Lady Boyd, from London, May 23, 1644, vol. 2. p. 314. (*vide*, chapter 3. reference 8).

56. *ibid.*

57. vol. 1. p. 303; *vide* also vol. 2. p. 117.

58. Carruthers, pp. 34-35.

59. *ibid.* p. 77; *vide* also Baillie, vol. 2. p. 238.

60. *ibid.* p. 77.

61. *ibid.* p. 75.

62. Hetherington, p. 159.

63. Lightfoot, pp. 255-56.
64. Gillespie, p. 13.
65. *ibid.* p. 29.
66. *ibid.* p. 32.
67. *Minutes.* p. 45.
68. *ibid.* p. 198.
69. *ibid.* p. 41.
70. *ibid.* p. 41.
71. *ibid.* p. 48.
72. Hetherington, p. 171; *vide* also Lightfoot, p. 231.
73. Lightfoot, pp. 230-233.
74. Baillie, vol. 2. p. 146.

Chapter 5

1. *vide* Bibliography of Rutherford's works.
2. *vide* Bibliography of Rutherford's sermons.
3. *A Free Disputation against Pretended Liberty of Conscience*, p. 370 (hereafter, Free Dis).
4. *Examen Arminianismi*, p. 130 (hereafter, Examen).
5. *ibid.* pp. 148-149.
6. *The Covenant of Life Opened*, pp. 31 and 34 (hereafter, Covenant).
7. *Influences of the Life of Grace*, pp. 34-35 (hereafter, Influences).
8. *ibid.* p. 40.
9. *Examen*, p. 335.
10. *Influences*, p. 32.
11. *ibid.* p. 141.
12. *Covenant*, p. 286.
13. *ibid.* p. 241.
14. *Examen*, p. 265.
15. *ibid.*
16. *ibid.*
17. *ibid.* p. 282.
18. *Covenant*, p. 314.
19. *ibid.* p. 239.
20. *ibid.* p. 288.
21. *Influences*, p. 235.
22. *Covenant*, p. 182.
23. *ibid.* p. 12.
24. *ibid.* pp. 346-47.
25. *ibid.* p. 233.
26. *vide* Bibliography, *Power and Prevalency of Faith and Prayer Evidenced,* p. 92, also *Covenant,* p. 202.
27. *Covenant*, p. 231.
28. *Examen*, p. 596.

29. *ibid.* p. 561.

30. *ibid.* p. 639.

31. *vide.* Bibliography, *The Divine Right of Government and Excommunication*, or a *Peaceable Dispute for the Perfection of the Holy Scripture in Point of Ceremonies and Church Government.* In this work the six books of Erastus against excommunication are briefly examined, with a vindication of Beza against the aspersions of Erastus. The due and just power of the magistrate in matters of religion, and the arguments of Prynne in so far as they agree with Erastus, are discussed. To this is added a brief *Tractate of Scandal*, answering the Doctors of Aberdeen. p. 42, also pp. 30-34 (hereafter *D.R.E.*).

32. Baillie,. vol. 2. p. 159.

33. *D.R.E.* p. 1

34. *ibid.* pp. 202-502.

35. *ibid.* p. 261.

36. *ibid.* p. 262.

37. *ibid.* p. 267..

38. *ibid.* p. 560.

39. *vide* Bibliography, *Due Right of Presbyteries, A Plea for the Government of the Church of Scotland.* In this: (i) is examined the way of the Church of Christ in New England in brotherly equality and independency or co-ordinations without subjection of one church to another; (ii) Their apology of this government, their answers to thirty two questions are considered; (iii) A treatise for a church government is discussed; (iv) The arguments of Mr. Robinson in his justification of separation are discussed, the power of the prince in matters ecclesiastical are considered, and various controversies resolved. Chap. I.

40. *Free Dis.* p. 36.

41. *ibid.* p. 41.

42. *Letters,* To Lady Kenmure, from Anwoth, June 28, 1636, vol. 2 p. 156 (*vide* chapter 2. reference 9).

43. *ibid.* To Lady Kenmure, from Anwoth, June 26, 1630, vol. I p.59.

44. *ibid.* To M.M. from Edinburgh, 1636 (undated), vol. I. p. 161.

45. *ibid.* To John Nevay, minister of New Mills, from Aberdeen, June 15, 1637, vol. 1. p. 246 (*vide* chapter 3, reference 49).

46. ibid. To Lady Kenmure, from London, March 4, 1644, vol. 2, p.312

47. *ibid.*

48. *ibid.*

49. *ibid.* To Lady Boyd, from London, May 25, 1644, vol. 2, p. 313.

50. *ibid.* To Lady Boyd, from St. Andrews, 1640, (undated) vol. 2. pp. 304-305.

51. *ibid.*

52. *ibid.* To Lady Boyd, from London, May 25, 1644, vol. 2. p. 313.

53. *ibid.*

54. James, I., *Political Works* (ed. C. H. McIlwain), Harvard University Press, Cambridge, Mass. 1918, p. 307.

55. Davies, G., p. 82.

56. *vide* Bibliography, *Lex Rex*. A dispute for the just prerogative of king and people containing the reasons and causes for the defensive wars of Scotland, and for help given to England. p. 45 (hereafter, *L.R.*).

57. Major, R. *History of Greater Britain*, Scot. Hist. Soc. Edinburgh, 1892, p. 214.

58. *ibid.* p. 215.

59. Row, W. *Life of Blair* (ed. by T. McCrie), Blackwood, Edinburgh 1848, p. 365.

60. *L.R.* Questions 28-37, pp. 257-383.

61. *ibid.* p. 165.

62. Published on July 4, 1644, printed in Bristol, possibly however an Oxford production, (*vide* Baillie, vol. 2. p. 207), re-published 1646, after Maxwell's death, under the title *Burden of Issachar.*

63. *Memoirs*, Oliphant, Edinburgh, 1748, p. 177.

64. *L.R.* p. 2.

65. *ibid.* p. 119.

66. *ibid.* pp. 46-48.

67. *Letters.* To Lady Boyd, from London, May 25, 1644 vol. 2. p. 315 (*vide* chapter 3 reference 2).

68. *L.R.* p. 123.

69. Act. 47, Parl. II, James VI, 1581.

70. *L.R.* p. 138.

71. *ibid.* pp. 333-35.

72. *ibid.* p. 141.

73. *ibid.* p. 163.

74. *ibid.* p. 158.

75. *ibid.* p. 179.

76. *Letters.* July 13, 1637, vol. 2, pp. 86-95: September 23, vol. 2, pp. 192-96.

77. *ibid.* To Lord Craighall, from Aberdeen, January 24, 1637, vol. 1, p. 219 (*vide* chapter 2, reference 52).

78. *ibid.* To Lord Lindsay of Byres, from Aberdeen, September 7, 1637, vol. 2, p. III. Lord Lindsay was the son of Robert, the ninth Lord Lindsay. He was born in 1596 and became Lord Lindsay on May 8, 1633. On July 23, 1644, he was appointed Lord High Treasurer of Scotland. Because of his support for the king at the time of the 'Engagement' in 1648, he was deprived of his offices by the Act of Classes and excluded from Parliament until Charles came to Scotland in 1650. He was censured too by the Church, but was restored by the General Assembly at Edinburgh in July, 1650. At

the Restoration he was restored to his offices. He died at Tyninghame in 1676. Rutherford's *Peaceable Plea for Paul's Presbytery in Scotland* was dedicated to him.

79. *ibid.* To Lord Loudon, from Aberdeen, January 4, 1638, vol. 2, p. 219. Lord Loudon was the son of Sir James Campbell. He was a strenuous opponent of attempts made by Charles I to impose Episcopacy. He was a member of the General Assembly which met at Glasgow in 1638. He commanded a brigade of horse in the fighting which followed. In 1641 he was appointed Lord Chancellor of Scotland. In 1650, he demitted office when the Malignants came to the fore, but continued to be a staunch supporter of Charles II, because of which he was exempted from Cromwell's Act of Indemnity and his estates forfeited. However he was not rewarded for his loyalty at the Restoration and feared he would suffer the fate of Argyll. He died on March 15, 1662. Rutherford dedicated to him his *Divine Right of Church Government and Excommunication.*

80. *ibid.* To the Earl of Cassillis, from Aberdeen, March 13, 1637, vol. 1, p. 311. The Earl of Cassillis was John Kennedy, son of Gilbert Kennedy, Master of Cassillis. He was a zealous Covenanter, although he opposed the taking up of arms against the king. He was a member of the Glasgow Assembly of 1638 and one of the elders who attended the Westminster Assembly in 1643. He attended the crowning of Charles II at Scone in 1651, and remained an opponent of Cromwell. He died in 1668.

81. *ibid.* To Lord Balmerinoch, from Aberdeen, March 1, 1637, vol. 1, p. 332. Lord Balmerinoch was John Elphinstone. He came into prominence when, in 1633, he opposed the imposition of Episcopacy. Soon after he was libelled and condemned to death for treason. However, after a long imprisonment he was given a reluctant pardon by the king, but continued his opposition to Charles I. He was a member of the Assembly of 1638. He died in 1649.

82. *ibid.* To Lord Craighall, from Aberdeen, July 8, 1637, vol. 2, p. 76 (*vide* chapter 2, reference 52).

83. *ibid.* To Lady Kenmure, from Aberdeen, August 10, 1637, vol. 2, p. 100 (*vide* chapter 2, reference 9).

84. *ibid.* To the Earl of Cassillis, from Aberdeen, 1637 (undated), vol. 2, p. 213 (*vide* this chapter, reference 80).

85. *ibid.* To the Laird of Carleton, from Aberdeen, March 14, 1637, vol. 1, p. 359. Bonar quotes Livingstone as saying there were two Carletons; the recipient of this letter was probably John Fullerton, in the parish of Borgue.

86. *ibid.* To Lord Boyd, from Aberdeen, 1637 (undated), vol. 1, p.199. Lord Boyd was the only son of Robert, sixth Lord Boyd. He died a young man in his twenties on November 17, 1640.

87. *ibid.* To M.M., from Aberdeen, January 3, 1637, vol. 1, p. 204 (*vide* chapter 2, reference 11).

88. *ibid.* To the Earl of Cassillis, from Aberdeen, September 9, 1637, vol. 2, p. 189 (*vide* this chapter reference 80).

89. *ibid.* pp. 48-49.

90. *ibid.* To M.M., from Anwoth, March 9, 1632, vol. 1, p. 93. As he also wrote to Lady Kenmure, from Anwoth, February 1, 1630, vol. 1, p. 55 (*vide* chapter 2, reference 9).

91. *ibid.* To M.M., from Anwoth, March 9, 1632, vol. 1, p. 93.

92. *ibid.* From Anwoth, 1634 (undated), vol. 1, p. 112 ff.

93. *ibid.* From Anwoth, 1630 (undated), vol. 1, pp. 54-56.

94. *ibid.* From Anwoth, June 2, 1631, vol. 1, p. 69; also from Anwoth, 1631 (undated) vol. 1, p. 74.

95. *ibid.* From Anwoth, 1630 (undated), vol. 1, p. 55.

96. *ibid.* vol. 1, p. 39; *vide* also *S.R.C.* pp. 29-34.

97. *ibid.* From Kirkcudbright, October 1, 1639, vol. 2, p. 347.

98. *ibid.* From Anwoth, February 1, 1630, vol. 1, p. 51.

99. *ibid.* From Anwoth, September 4, 1629, vol. 1, p. 46.

100. *ibid.* vol. 1, pp. 39, 80, 90, 102, 114, 128.

101. *ibid.* vol. 1, p. 197 (*vide S.R.C.* pp. 50-58, also chapter 3, reference 8).

102. *ibid.* From Aberdeen, 1637 (undated), vol. 1, p. 197.

103. *ibid.* From Aberdeen, March 7, 1637, vol. 1, p. 272.

104. *ibid.* From Aberdeen, May 1, 1637, vol. 8, pp. 390-97.

105. *ibid.* From Edinburgh, July 30, 1636, vol. 1, p. 165 (*vide* chapter 3, reference 46).

106. *ibid.* From Aberdeen, February 20, 1637, vol. 1, p. 255.

107. *ibid.* From Aberdeen, 1637 (undated), vol. 2, p. 196. Lady Largirie was the wife of the proprietor of Castlemadie, in the Stewartry of Kirkcudbright. The place was also called Largero, or Largerie in the parish of Tynholm.

108. *ibid.* From Aberdeen, 1637 (undated), vol. 2, p. 196. Lady Busbie was probably the mother-in-law of Robert Blair, Rutherford's friend. Blair married Catherine, daughter of Hugh Montgomery, Laird of Busbie.

109. *ibid.* From Aberdeen, September 7, 1637, vol. 2, p. 138. Lady Rowallan was before marriage Sarah Brisbane, the fourth daughter of John Brisbane of Bishoptoun, and the third wife of Sir William Mure of Rowallan.

110. *ibid.* From Aberdeen, March 13, 1637, vol. 1, p. 33. Lady Mar, the Younger, was before her marriage Christian Hay, the daughter of Francis, the ninth Earl of Errol. She was the wife of the eighth Earl of Mar.

111. *ibid.* From Aberdeen, March 14, 1637, vol. 1, p. 346. Lady Hallhill was the wife of Sir James Melville of Hallhill in Fife.

112. *ibid.* From Aberdeen, September 7, 1637, vol. 2, p. 131. Lady Gaitgirth, née Isabel Blair, daughter of John Blair, was the wife of James Chalmers of Gaitgirth.

113. *ibid.* From Aberdeen, September 10, 1637, vol. 2, p. 169. (*vide* this chapter, reference 77).

114. *ibid.* From Aberdeen, 1637 (undated), vol. 2, p. 159. Lady Dungueigh was Sarah, sister of M.M. She was married to Samuel Lockhard, merchant burgess in Edinburgh.

115. *ibid.* From Aberdeen, August 8, 1637, vol. 2, p. 95. Lady Kilconquhair was Helen, the third daughter of Sir Archibald Murray of Blackbarony, and the wife of Sir John Carstairs of Kilconquhair in Fife.

116. *ibid.* From Aberdeen, 1637 (undated), vol. 1, p. 201.

117. *ibid.* From Aberdeen, March 13, 1637, vol. 1, pp. 318-319, also from Aberdeen, March 14, 1637, vol. 1, p. 354.

118. *ibid.* From Aberdeen, November 22, 1636, vol. 1, p. 184. M'Kail was minister in Irvine. His nephew, also Hugh, was martyred in 1666.

119. *ibid.* From Aberdeen, March 7, 1637, vol. 1, p. 276.

120. *ibid.* From Aberdeen, 1637 (undated), vol. 1, p. 297.

121. *ibid.* 1651 (undated), also no indication of where written. It appears from a Wodrow postscript that the minister had been deposed by the Resolutioners (*vide* following chapter for Protester-Resolutioner controversy). Probably he had been censured by the Dundee Assembly of 1651 for his opposition to the public Resolutions. Three ministers were deposed by that Assembly, one being from Glasgow, Patrick Gillespie, who seems to have been the recipient of this letter. He was the son of John Gillespie, second minister of the Collegiate charge of Kirkcaldy. He was born at Kirkcaldy in 1617, and was for some time minister of that parish, prior to his translation to Glasgow. He was a supporter of Cromwell, and appointed by the Protector Principal of Glasgow University. At the Restoration he was ejected from the post, imprisoned in Edinburgh and thereafter Stirling. In 1661 he was impeached for high treason, but was shortly freed and confined to Ormiston.

122. *ibid.* From St. Andrews, February 15, 1661, vol. 2, p. 417. Guthrie was martyred in 1661.

123. *ibid.* From Aberdeen, February 7, 1637, vol. 1, pp. 233-34.

124. *ibid.*

125. *ibid.* From Aberdeen, 1637 (undated), vol. 2, p. 22.

126. *ibid.* From Aberdeen, July 7, 1637, vol. 2, p. 64.

127. *ibid.* vol. 1, p. 139.

128. *ibid.* vol. 1, p. 116.

129. *ibid.* vol. 1, p. 125.

130. *ibid.*

131. *ibid.* vol. 1, p. 131.

132. *ibid.* vol. 1, p. 137.

133. Chambers, W. and R. *Encyclopaedia of English Literature,* London and Edinburgh, 1903, vol. 1, p. 504.

134. *op. cit.* p. 2.

135. Davies, G. *op. cit.* p. 165 (from Letter 136, Carlyle 2, p. 79), August 3, 1650.

136. Donne, J., Holy Sonnet 18.

137. Fuller, T. *Holy State Book*, Cambridge University Press, 1921. vol. 2, chapter 6.

138. Hobbes, T. *Leviathan* (ed. Lindsay, A.D.), Dent and Sons, London, 1928. vol. 4, p. 298.

139. *Letters*. From Aberdeen, 1637 (undated), vol. 1, p. 298.

140. *ibid.* To a Gentlewoman from Aberdeen, 1637 (undated), vol. 1, p. 303. To Rob. Lennox, from Aberdeen, 1637 (undated), vol. 2, p.60. We know little of Lennox. His name often occurs in the minute book of the committee of the Covenanters. He is said to be of Disdove, which is a farm about a mile from Girthan.

141. *ibid.* To Viscountess Kenmure, from Edinburgh, July 28, 1636.

142. *ibid.* From Anwoth, January 15, 1629, vol. 1, p. 48.

143. *ibid.* to M.M., from Anwoth, February 11, 1631, vol. 1, p. 65, (*vide* chapter 2, reference 11).

144. *ibid.* From Anwoth, September 14, 1629, vol. 1, p. 48.

145. *ibid.* To M.M., from Edinburgh, December (undated), 1634, vol. 1, p. 139.

146. *ibid.* To M.M., from Anwoth, 1636 (undated), vol. 1, p. 150.

147. *ibid.* From Anwoth, 1634 (undated), vol. 1, p. 138.

148. *ibid.* From Aberdeen, September 21, 1636, vol. 1, pp. 175-176.

149. *ibid.* To Lady Culross, from Aberdeen, December 30, 1636, vol. 1, p. 190.

150. *ibid.* To Lady Kenmure, from Anwoth, September 14, 1634, vol. 1, p. 177, ff. (*vide* chapter 2, reference 9).

151. *ibid.* To Jean Brown, from Aberdeen, 1637 (undated), vol. 1, p. 215. Jean Brown was the mother of John Brown, minister of Wamphray, Annandale.

Chapter 6

1. *Letters*. From St. Andrews, June 30th, 1649, vol. 2, p. 347.

2. *Records*. February 18th, 1648, vol. 2, p. 360.

3. *ibid.* February 21st, 1648, vol. 2, p. 360.

4. *ibid.* February 28th, 1648, vol. 2, p. 361.

5. *ibid.* May 1st, 1648, vol. 2, p. 513.

6. *ibid.* August 11th, 1648, vol. 25, p. 4.

7. *ibid.* December 11th, 1649, vol. 25, p. 310.

8. *ibid.* September, 1649, vol. 25, p. 35.

9. *ibid.* vol. 2, p. 179.

10. *ibid.* vol. 2, p. 202.

172   Samuel Rutherford

172   Samuel Rutherford

11. *ibid.* vol. 1, p. 138.

12. Baillie, 3.33 ff., also *Records.* vol. 1, p. 372.

13. *Records*: vol. 1, pp. 377-382.

14. *ibid.* vol. 1, p. 387.

15. *ibid.* vol. 1, p. 389-390.

16. *ibid.* vol. 1, p. 48.

17. *ibid.* vol. 1, pp. 529-531.

18. *ibid.* (Coupar) 1648, vol. 2, p. 114.

19. Gardiner, S.R. (ed). *Charles II and Scotland, 1650*, Scot. Hist. Soc., Edinburgh, 1894, September 25th, 1649. (hereafter, *C. and S.*)

20. *ibid. A Letter from Paris*, January 30th, 1650; also February 27th, 1650, pp. 6 and 16.

21. *ibid.* From Stockholm, January 26th, 1650, p. 10; Letter from Henry May to Secretary Nicholas, March 30th, p. 49.

22. *ibid. A Letter from Paris*, February 12th, 1650, p. 8.

23. *ibid. A Letter from Breda*, May 16-26, 1650, p. 109.

24. *ibid. A Letter from Paris,* April 13-23, 1650, p. 66.

25. *ibid. A Letter from the Prince of Orange*, April 17-27, 1650, p. 69.

26. *ibid. Letter*, May 26th, 1650, p. 106.

27. *ibid. Letter from Beauvais*, February 28th, 1649, p. 19.

28. *ibid. Conversations with the Dean of Tuam*, August 20th, 1650, p. 74.

29. *ibid.* p. 142.

30. *ibid. A Letter from Breda*, April 21st - May 1st, 1650, p. 74.

31. Baillie. vol. 3, pp. 115-18.

32. *ibid.* vol. 3, p. 118.

33. *C. and S.* Letter from Perty, November 23rd, 1650.

34. *Records of the Commissions of the General Assembly of the Church of Scotland*, Scot. Hist. Soc. Edinburgh 1892, vol. 2, p. 158.

35. *ibid.*

36. *ibid.* vol. 3, p. 345.

37. *ibid.* vol. 3, p. 361.

38. Row: pp. 264 and 269.

39. Baillie. vol. 3, p. 126.

40. Warriston, A. *Diary, 1632-1639* (ed. Johnston, A.), Edin. Univ. Press, Edinburgh 1911 (hereafter – Warriston).

41. Row. p. 275.

42. *ibid.* p. 277.

43. *ibid.* pp. 84-86.

44. *ibid.* p. 86. Row, p. 279.

45. Warriston, p. 140.

46. Ogilvie, J. D. *Resolutioner - Protester Controversy,* Transactions of the Edinburgh Bibliographical Society 1930, vol. 4, p. 330.

47. *op. cit.* vol. 3, pp. 313-14.

48. *op. cit.* vol. 45, p. 14.

49. *Letters.* (undated) 1651, vol. 2, p. 376.

50. Balfour, J. *Annals*, Aitchison, Edinburgh, 1824, vol. 4, p. 330.

51. Baillie. vol. 3, pp. 288, 318, 387.

52. Row. p. 318.

53. Firth, C. H. *Scotland and the Protectorate*, University of Edinburgh Press, Edinburgh, 1895, November 10th, 1654, from Dalkeith, p. 33 (hereafter, *S. and P.*).

54. Warriston. vol. 2, p. 305.

55. Baillie. vol. 3, pp. 243, 249, 281.

56. Firth, C. H. *Scotland under the Commonwealth*, University of Edinburgh Press Edinburgh, 1985, p. LIX.

57. *S. and P.* p. 280.

58. *ibid.* LVIII.

59. *ibid.* Letter from Lilburne to Cromwell, Dalkeith, March 16th, 1654, p. LVII.

60. Baillie. vol. 3, p. 280.

61. *ibid.* vol. 3, p. 297.

62. *ibid.* vol. 3, p. 296.

63. *Consultations of the Ministers of Edinburgh*, 1632-1660, Scottish History Society, Rev. W. Stephenson, Edinburgh University Press, Edinburgh, vol. 1, p. 354, 1921 (hereafter, Consultations).

64. *ibid.* vol. 2, p. 140.

65. *ibid.* vol. 2, p. 192.

66. *Letters.* To John Murray, from St. Andrews, January 25th, 1660, vol. 2, p. 405. John Murray was a Protester, the minister of Methven. He was imprisoned in Edinburgh Castle for meeting with others to draw up a congratulatory address to Charles II at his restoration, expressing their loyalty and reminding him of the obligation of the Covenant. He was charged with high treason, but at length was liberated. In about 1672 he was imprisoned again, this time in the Tolbooth of Edinburgh, for holding house conventicles. Again he was released but confined to the parish of Queensferry and ordered to abstain from conventicles and attend the parish church.

67. *Consultations*: vol. 2, p. 175.

68. Preface to *Joshua Redivivus.*

69. Record of the Kirk Session, St. Andrews, May 3rd, 1643.

70. Murray, p. 247.

71. Baillie, vol. 3, p. 295.

72. Bower, A. *History of Edinburgh University*, Oliphant, Waugh and Innes, Edinburgh, 1817, vol. 1, pp. 206-252.

73. McLeod, J. *Scottish Theology*, Edinburgh 1943, p. 74.

74. Balfour, vol. 3, p. 413.

75. *Letters*. To John Murray (*vide* above reference 66) from St. Andrews, June 25th, 1660, vol. 2, p. 405.

76. *ibid*. From St. Andrews, June 25th, 1660, vol. 2, pp. 357-358.

77. *ibid*. From St. Andrews (undated), 1660, vol. 2, p. 412.

Chapter 7

1. *Letters*. From Aberdeen, 1st May, 1637, vol. 1, p. 393.

2. *ibid*.

3. Hetherington. p. 141

4. Baillie. vol. 1, p. 450.

5. Innes, Taylor. A.,. 'Samuel Rutherford,' *Studies in Scottish History*, London, 1892.

6. *Covenant*. p. 140.

7. Jones, R. *Studies in Mystical Religion*, Macmillan, London, 1909, p.447.

8. Rutherford, S. *Survey of the Spiritual Antichrist*, p. 13.

9. *Letters*. To Thomas Garven, from Aberdeen, 1637. (undated), vol. 1, p. 386. Thomas Garven was a minister of Edinburgh. He was banished from the city in 1662, by the king, for his Presbyterian principles.

10. *ibid*. From Aberdeen, September 11th, 1637, vol. 2, p. 176.

11. *ibid*. From Anwoth, September 14th, 1634, vol. 1, p. 118.

12. *ibid*. From Aberdeen, March 13th, 1637, vol. 1, p. 318.

13. *ibid*. From Aberdeen, 1637 (undated), vol. 1, p. 242.

14. *ibid*. From Aberdeen, July 13th, 1637, vol. 2, p. 88.

15. *ibid*. From Anwoth, April 1st, 1633, vol. 1, p. 102. *vide* also to John Livingstone from Aberdeen, February 7th, 1637, vol. 1, p. 234. John Livingstone was the son of Alexander Livingstone, first minister of Kilsyth, and later of Lanark. John was the first minister of Killinchy in Ireland in 1630. He was suspended by the Bishop of Down for non-conformity, after less than a year's ministry. Later he was excommunicated, but in 1638 he became minister of Stranraer until 1648, when he was translated by the General Assembly to Ancrum. In 1649 he was sent to the Hague and later to Breda as a commissioner to treat with Charles II. In the Resolutioner-Protester controversy, he belonged to the latter party. At the Restoration in 1660 he was exiled from Scotland, finding refuge in Rotterdam, where he remained until his death in 1672.

16. *ibid*. From Anwoth, September 14th, 1629, vol. 1, p. 47.

17. *ibid*. From Anwoth, September 14th, 1634, vol. 1, pp. 317-318.

18. *ibid*. To John Kennedy from Anwoth, February 2nd, 1632, (*vide* chapter 4, reference 18) vol. 1, p. 89.

19. *S.R.C*. pp. 26 and 28.

20. *Letters*. To John Kennedy, from Aberdeen, vol. 1, pp. 192-193. (*vide* chapter 4, reference 18).

21. *ibid.* From Aberdeen, February 16th, 1637, vol. 1, p. 247 (*vide* chapter 2, reference 50).

22. *ibid.* From Aberdeen, February 19th, 1637, vol. 1, p. 250.

23. *ibid.* From Aberdeen, February 20th, 1637, vol. 1, p. 253.

24. *ibid.* From Aberdeen, March 7th, 1637, vol. 2, p. 276.

25. *Tryal and Triumph of Faith and Prayer*: p. 6.

26. *Letters*. From Aberdeen, January 1st, 1637, vol. 1, pp. 195-196.

27. *ibid.* To John Kennedy, June 3rd, 1637, vol. 1, p. 193. John Kennedy was the son of Ayr's Provost.

28. *ibid.* To Bethsaida Aird, from Aberdeen, March 14th, 1637, vol. 1, p. 354. Bethsaida Aird was a parishioner of Anwoth.

29. Romans 7:24.

30. *Letters*. From Aberdeen, September 23rd, 1637, vol. 2, p. 193.

31. *ibid.* To Rutherford's parishioners, from Aberdeen, July 13th, 1637, vol. 2, p. 89.

32. *ibid.* March 4th, 1644, vol. 2, p. 311.

33. *ibid.* To Lady Boyd, from London, May 25th, 1644, vol. 2, p.313 (*vide* chapter 3, reference 8).

34. *ibid.* To Lady Boyd, from St. Andrews, 1640 (undated), vol. 2, p. 304.

35. Ordination debate at Westminster, March 18th, 1644. Lightfoot, p. 231: debate of April, 16th, 1644, pp. 255-256.

36. Ross, J. *A History of Congregational Independency in Scotland*, Maclehose, Glasgow, 1900, p. 21.

37. Peterkin. Act of the Assembly of 1647, p. 476.

38. *Letters*. To Lady Kenmure, March 4th, 1644, vol. 2, p. 311.

39. Gilmour. p. 204.

40. Fisher, H.A.L. *History of the Church*, Hodder and Stoughton, London, 1887, p. 466.

Persons' Index

Subject Index